LANDSCAPING
Your HOME

fine
Gardening Design Guides

LANDSCAPING
Your HOME

Creative Ideas *from* America's Best Gardeners

The Taunton Press

Special thanks to the editors, art directors, copy editors, and other staff members of Fine Gardening *who contributed to the development of the articles featured in this book.*

Front cover photographers: © J. Paul Moore (large); Lee Anne White, © The Taunton Press, Inc. (inset)
Back cover photographers: © John Glover (large); author photos courtesy *Fine Gardening* magazine, © The Taunton Press, Inc.
Publisher: Jim Childs
Acquisitions Editor: Lee Anne White
Editorial Assistant: Meredith DeSousa
Technical Editor: Todd Meier
Copy Editor: Candace Levy
Indexer: Linda Stannard
Art Director: Paula Schlosser
Design Manager: Rosalind Wanke
Cover & Interior Designer: Lori Wendin
Layout Artists: Carol Petro, Rosalie Vaccaro

Taunton
BOOKS & VIDEOS
for fellow enthusiasts

Printed in the United States of America
10 9 8 7 6 5 4 3 2 1

The Taunton Press, Inc., 63 South Main Street, PO Box 5506,
Newtown, CT 06470-5506
e-mail: tp@taunton.com

Distributed by Publishers Group West

Library of Congress Cataloging-in-Publication Data
Landscaping your home : creative ideas from America's best gardeners.
p. cm.–(Fine gardening design guides)
ISBN 1-56158-471-1
1. Landscape gardening. 2. Gardens—Design. 3. Landscape gardening—United States.
4. Gardens—United States—Design. I. Fine gardening. II. Series.
SB473.L373   2001
712'6—dc21   00-59933

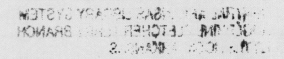

> "*The size of your property doesn't matter. It may be a small city lot or a rural spread. But it's yours, and you want to do something to it.*"
>
> —Sydney Eddison,
> *The Self-Taught Gardener*

Contents

Introduction

There are many reasons to landscape your home. Some are practical: Perhaps you've just built a new home and are surrounded by a sea of fill dirt. Or you've just moved into a house with overgrown foundation plantings and no clear path to the front door. Maybe, after many years in the same home, it's simply time to update your landscape. Or it could be the sale of your home that's driving a fix-up—after all, you know what the real-estate professionals say about curb appeal.

Other reasons for landscaping your home may be borne of passion: You're an avid gardener and want more space for growing perennials. You love rooms filled with fresh flowers and desire a cutting garden. You enjoy entertaining outdoor, and want to create an intimate terrace garden for evening gatherings. Your children need a comfortable and safe place to play where you can keep an eye on them from the kitchen window. Or you need a quiet refuge and are seeking ways to make your home feel private and serene.

Whatever the reason, *Landscaping Your Home* will help you evaluate your property, design the garden spaces you've been dreaming about, take a practical approach to problem areas, and create outdoor living areas that suit your family's lifestyle. You can count on hands-on advice from some of America's best gardeners to guide you along the way—landscape and garden designers that speak from years of experience. For years, they've been sharing their insights in *Fine Gardening* magazine. Now, you have their work in a single book that you can take with you out in the yard for inspiration and ideas.

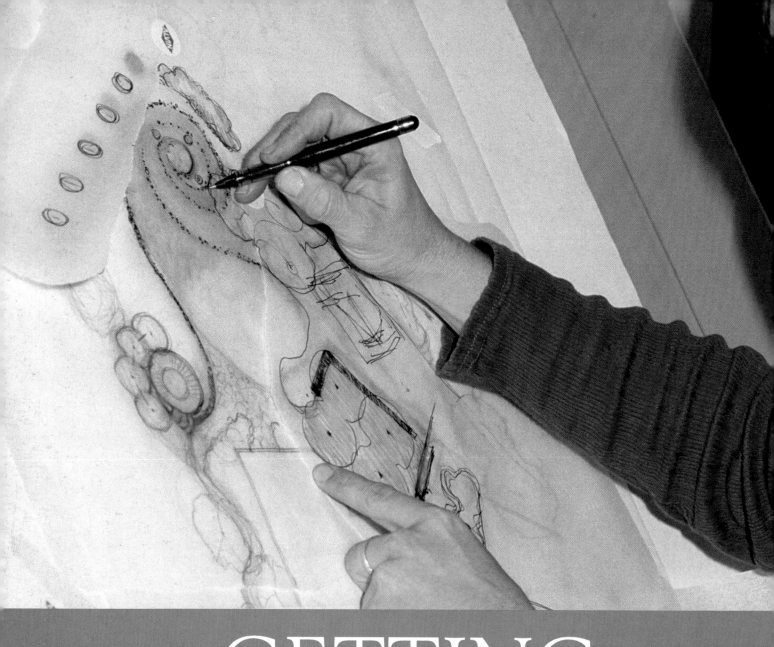

GETTING
STARTED

1

PERHAPS THE HARDEST PART of any landscaping job is just getting started. After all, at this stage in the game, there are so many possibilities. Should you turn your place into a cottage garden, a naturalistic garden, or a formal garden? How will you use your space—for family activities, outdoor entertaining, or a quiet refuge? Will brick, stone, cobbles, or concrete look best for your pathways? And where will that perennial border you've been dreaming about go?

Designers know that there is as much logic to garden design as there is creativity. That's why they recommend that you start with a plan. And in this section, you'll learn how to go about creating that plan—whether you work with a design professional or do it all yourself. You'll learn how design ideas originate, how to evaluate your site and draw a base map, and how to explore your dreams by creating a concept plan. You'll even find out what it takes to keep up with an ever-changing garden.

What to Do before You Draw

LEE ANNE WHITE

is consulting editor and the former editor of *Fine Gardening*. She is a Master Gardener and has studied garden design at various schools, workshops, and conferences.

Measure everything and mark it on a map. Don't stop at the property lines. You want to measure it all—driveways, sidewalks, outbuildings, doors, windows, utilities, faucets, trees, and planting beds. Jot down all measurements on a rough sketch of your site.

WRITERS START WITH a blank sheet of paper. Artists with a clear canvas. So, it reasons, a landscape designer should begin with a bare lot. But that's rarely the case. Even on a new construction site, you have differing light conditions, changes in grade, varied soil conditions, and usually at least a few plants. And it's for precisely these reasons that a landscape designer must be part horticulturist, part construction manager, and part creative genius.

With so many considerations, I've often wondered just how a designer approaches a new project. How much of the process is purely creative, and how much is simply pragmatic? Do designers have a bag of tricks from which they draw their ideas and inspiration? And what information do they need to gather together before they can sit down at the drawing table?

Snapshots can be revealing. Sometimes cameras see what the eyes overlook. Be sure to photograph the yard, the house, and the views from both. These site photos will be helpful when you're back at the drawing table.

So like a college student heading off for a day on the job with a professional in my chosen field of study, I hopped a plane for California to hook up with landscape architect Jeni Webber. I was going to watch her go through the paces—from an initial site visit, to the client meeting, and on to the rounds of drawing-table revisions that would result in a concept plan for the owners of a new home—to see what I could learn about the process of landscape design. As it turns out, Jeni took a step-by-step approach to the project that gave her a framework for planning and jump-started the creative process.

SURVEY THE SITE WITH A CRITICAL EYE

Our first stop was the clients' home. David and Jody Suchard live in a new subdivision in St. Helena, California, in the heart of the Napa Valley wine country. It was the

Suchards' first house, and they had moved in only three months earlier. The building contractor had installed a few shrubs and trees in the front yard, as he had done for the other houses on the street, but the backyard, at least in the torrential rains we faced that day, was a large expanse of mucky clay. A fence surrounded the yard, keeping the dog in bounds, but otherwise, there wasn't a tree trunk or blade of grass to be found.

As the weather broke and the skies briefly cleared, we headed out to evaluate the property and take measurements. Jeni took notes, roughly sketched the site on her oversized clipboard, and talked with the Suchards—occasionally putting them to work holding the tape measure. She noted that the soil was soggy, but not beyond reason, considering the 5 in. of rain that had fallen during the past 24 hours. The property was mostly flat, sloping slightly to a then-raging creek just beyond the fence line, so drainage was not a major problem. Even so, she noted that more grade was needed in some areas to keep water from puddling.

From the back door, you could see a half-dozen rooftops over the far fence (a view that needed screening) and a beautiful grove of oaks over the fence to the right (a view to preserve). She observed that there wasn't a clear path from the house to the freestanding garage, and that this property was far from being rectangular. In fact, it had more nooks, crannies, and diagonal property lines than any yard I'd seen.

Jeni pulled out her tape measure, verified the numbers on the plat (a map showing the house and property lines) provided by the builder, and added a few of her own measurements. In addition to checking the property boundaries and how they related to the house, garage, driveway, and sidewalk, she measured the doors and windows, marking the views and entries on her plans, and indicated the placement of utilities such as the air conditioner and faucets for hoses. Downspouts were also noted, so drain lines could be run away from the house. The plat showed power and gas lines, but Jeni said she'd call to verify their placement before sinking a shovel in the ground.

Along one edge of the property there was a sharp rise of several feet, so she measured the grade and made a note on her sketch. Jeni then pulled out a compass, checked for true north, and made notations about the shade that would be created on the property at different times of day and through the seasons. There weren't any trees yet, but there would be plenty of shade cast by houses and fences. If there had been existing trees, shrubs, massed plantings, or other structures, she would have sketched them in as well. And although the homeowners already had a solid fence outside the bedroom window, she made a few notes about privacy needs.

Finally, we took photographs of the site—mud puddles and all. This included shooting all the nooks and crannies, as well as the views. We also photographed the house in its setting, and details of the architecture and building materials. Since the house had a stacked-stone foundation, a photograph would be helpful when it came to selecting complementary hardscaping materials at the stoneyard.

HOMEOWNER PREFERENCES ARE A TOP PRIORITY

Back inside, Jeni engaged the Suchards in conversation to find out more about their personal interests, as well as their landscaping needs. Later, she confided in me that she had also made general observations about their home for clues about their decorating tastes, favorite colors, and personal interests.

Jeni spread out a big stack of books, color swatches, and her laptop computer on the dining-room table. These were used to encourage discussion and to help Jeni get a feel for

"Conversations revolved around how the Suchards wanted to use the space and what ideas they already had for the property."

Installing a Landscape in Phases

Few are blessed with unrestricted budgets or the time to install an entire landscape at once. Which is why most homeowners choose to implement a landscape plan in phases. Here are landscape architect Jeni Webber's thoughts on the subject:

FINE GARDENING: What are the advantages of creating an overall concept plan even when you can't install it all immediately?

WEBBER: A concept plan lets you think long-term about your property—to consider the "big picture." But just because you're thinking about the finished landscape does not mean you have to install it all at once. By installing a landscape in phases, you can better manage your expenses and do much of the hands-on work yourself.

FG: What part of the process do your clients usually handle?

WEBBER: Most gardeners choose to do their own planting, especially since most plants come in 1-, 5-, and 15-gallon containers. Big trees or heavy shrubs are best left to the contractors. Amending soil, spreading mulch, and installing drip irrigation are also projects homeowners can tackle. Some, depending on their time and skills, also help build stone walls, install brick walks, or even build decks. It's important to be realistic about your schedule and abilities, or you'll just get frustrated with the work.

FG: What projects should be completed the first year?

WEBBER: Lawns, trees, and certain hardscaping features like patios or retaining walls usually come first. Lawns give children a place to play and provide a ground cover; trees need the longest time to get established; and, for practical reasons, many hardscaping features need to be installed before gardens are planted. Homeowners typically start in the front yard, then move to the back. An area for sitting outdoors is often a top priority. It's also important to take care of grading projects and to install any utilities very early in the process. I also like to get a head start on amending the soil for beds and borders. One trick I've learned is to decide where you'll get the most bang for your buck. An example is planting vines: They're inexpensive, grow quickly, and can give your place a lived-in look in a single season.

FG: How does installing a landscape in phases affect the design process?

WEBBER: The main thing to keep in mind is providing access where you need it. If you'll need to get a backhoe or other large equipment in the backyard at some point, make sure you don't design and install permanent structures like fences or retaining walls that would keep you from getting there. You can also plan for long-range changes—like converting a play area to a lap pool once children have grown.

Take lots of notes as you discuss family needs, design styles, color preferences, and initial ideas. They will jog your memory as you design. Books, color swatches, *The Color Star*, and plant encyclopedias are all tools for fostering conversation.

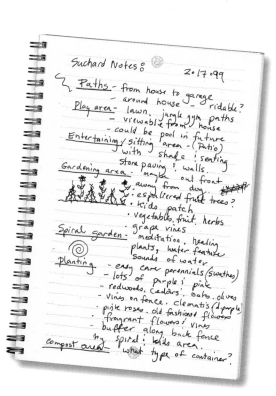

what interested her clients. She showed photographs of all styles of gardens, paying careful attention to Jody and David's "oohs" and "aahs." She noted when a photograph reminded Jody of her mother's garden. And although Jody and David said they didn't really have any color preferences, Jody mentioned more than a few times how much she loved the lavender blossoms of wisteria and "that dark purple clematis." She also migrated toward the pinks and purples when Jeni pulled out her color swatches and *The Color Star,* a nifty tool created by Johannes Itten for evaluating color combinations.

Conversations revolved around how the Suchards wanted to use the space and what ideas they already had for the property. They had a 2-year-old son, plus a second child on the way, so play space that could be viewed from the house was important. They needed a place for the jungle gym that had already been ordered, some lawn for playing games, and paths for riding tricycles and bikes.

Because David is a doctor, they wanted a healing garden, and batted around ideas for a spiral garden filled with herbs and a bench for meditation. The Suchards also love to entertain and requested a shaded patio for parties on warm summer days. And because they planned to add an atrium bathroom to the house, they expressed concerns about privacy and wanted to create an intimate setting.

To create a sense of place, draw from the local landscape. If you want your place to fit in, you have to look beyond your garden walls for inspiration. In the Napa Valley, grape arbors, silver-foliaged trees and plants, cypress hedges, and stone walls are common landscape elements that could be echoed in a garden.

An Analysis Diagram Shows Attributes As Well As Problems

A site-analysis diagram shows what's on the site at the outset. It should note measurements, drainage problems, circulation, views, and light conditions.

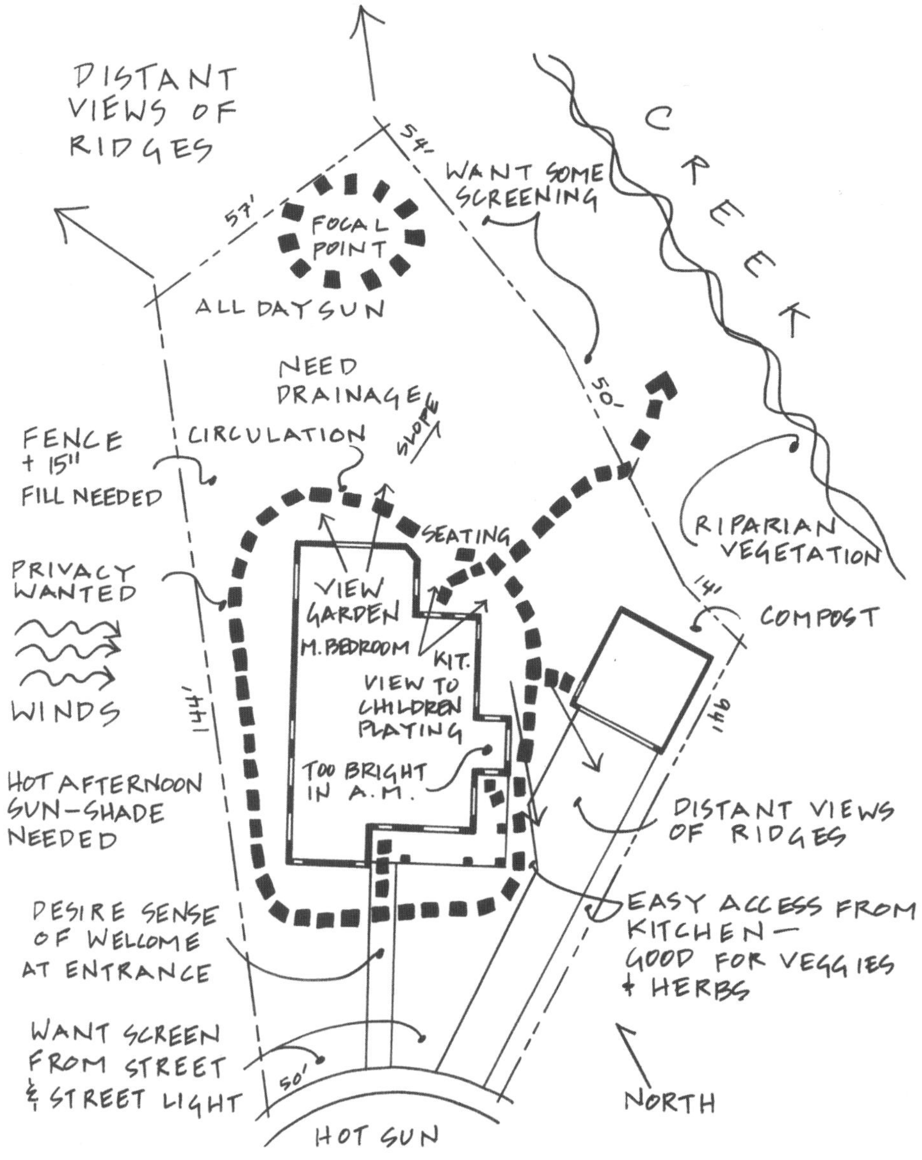

On a more practical note, the Suchards needed better access from the front yard to the back; a way to get from the house to the garage; and a convenient yet obscured place for the trash cans and the compost pile. For safety reasons, they were concerned about neighborhood children playing beside the creek, and requested a hedge or some type of barrier to discourage foot and bike traffic.

To talk more about plants, Jeni pulled out her laptop computer, inserted a CD (*Horticopia*), and showed the Suchards photographs of plants that grew well in their northern California climate. Although neither had much gardening experience, Jody wanted a place to grow flowers and vegetables. David was more interested in trees. So after mulling over favorite annuals, perennials, and vegetables, they turned the conversation to redwoods, oaks, and olives. Together, they decided to go with a mix of natives and low-maintenance exotics to keep yard work to a minimum except in the flower and vegetable gardens.

Budgets and time frames were also discussed. The Suchards had an overall budget figure they felt was appropriate for the home and their financial situation, but noted that they might not be able to spend this amount all at once. Jeni reassured them that this was not a problem, adding that it is nice to have a master plan that can be implemented in phases. Because this was their first home, they wanted a plan that would increase their property value and could be installed over two or three years, rather than opting for a 5- or 10-year plan.

TAKE A CLOSE LOOK AT THE LOCAL LANDSCAPE

Both Jeni and her clients had an interest in creating a sense of place—making the house and garden look as if they truly belonged in the Napa Valley. So we rode around the neighborhood; through the small downtown district; and along the winding back roads that passed orchards, olive groves, and vineyards.

Naturally, a few grape vines would be in order, but Jeni took note of the preponderance of silver-foliaged plants, the scrub-oak hedgerows, the rows of cypress that lined so many driveways, and the masses of an ornamental grass that were thriving in front of a local restaurant. While not all of these were native to California, they epitomized the vernacular landscape, reminiscent of France, Italy, and even Spain.

Jeni also sought out common hardscaping features, taking particular note of stone-wall construction, fence styles, and local colors. There was also the bungalow style of architecture that dominated the town and was reflected even in the Suchards' contemporary home.

"Both Jeni and her clients had an interest in creating a sense of place—making the house and garden look as if they truly belonged in the Napa Valley."

All of these elements would be considered when selecting plants and hardscaping materials for the project.

MAKE A SKETCH THAT SHOWS WHAT YOU'VE GOT

After wrapping up our site visit and client meeting, and exploring a bit of the wine country, we loaded up the truck and headed south for Jeni's studio in Oakland. Although she immediately began working at the drawing table, it still wasn't time to design. But it was time to draw, and an analysis diagram was the first sketch she made.

An analysis diagram is a base map drawn to scale with notes gathered during the site visit. It includes the property lines, house, street, sidewalk, driveway, outbuildings, and existing plantings. It also indicates the views, utilities, grade changes, sunny and shady areas, drainage problems, and screening needs of the property.

In other words, it is what's there originally—both the good and the bad. Armed with an analysis diagram and an understanding of the clients' needs and preferences, Jeni is ready to shift gears to the creative design process. She can begin to ponder solutions to drainage and access problems; to identify areas for entertaining, gardening, and other family activities; and to create interesting views from the home's interior. It's here where the real fun—creating a concept plan—begins.

LEE ANNE WHITE

is consulting editor and the former editor of *Fine Gardening.* She is a Master Gardener and has studied garden design at various schools, workshops, and conferences.

A Concept Plan

Pulls It All Together

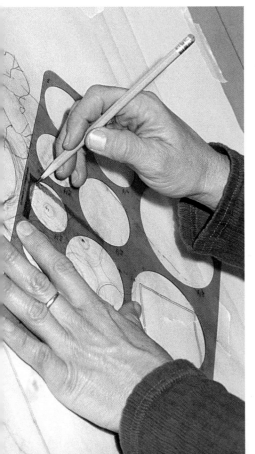

(FAR LEFT) In the studio, landscape architect Jeni Webber starts by sketching out rough ideas. Fine-tuning will be done later in the process.

(INSET) By working in pencil, it's easy to make minor changes. Trees were first sketched on the plan by hand. Then a template is used to more accurately note the mature size of sycamores that will be planted in the patio area.

"I MUST BE NUTS," I mumbled to myself as I boarded the plane for Oakland. Would it really be possible to get a feel for the creative process a landscape architect goes through to design a landscape plan? After all, landscape architects spend years learning their craft. And without a degree in psychology, I figured I'd never really understand how the creative mind works.

Even so, I did make a surprising discovery during my week with landscape architect Jeni Webber: The process she goes through to develop a concept plan for a client is strikingly similar to the process I go through to write a magazine article. First, there's the research, or in this case, the site analysis. Then the material is organized; a rough draft, or plan, is created; and rounds of revisions are made. Finally, the work is polished and presented.

As we moved into the studio for the creative phase of this project—a design for David and Jody Suchard's property in the Napa Valley—I did my best not to make many

A bubble diagram is like a working outline; it gives a sense of organization to the design project. Jeni played with some rough ideas on a napkin over lunch, made changes, and then drew a working diagram on drafting paper.

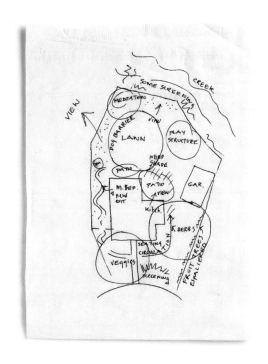

comments, as I didn't want to influence the process or outcome. Instead, I took notes and snapped lots of pictures. In the end, she got her concept plan, and I got my story.

A SIMPLE BUBBLE DIAGRAM HELPS ORGANIZE THE SPACE

With a site analysis completed, notes from the client meeting tucked away in her sketch book, and a few ideas kicking around in her head, Jeni started drawing. Only she wasn't in her studio. We were at lunch, and she was sketching what she called a "bubble diagram" on her napkin.

After roughly sketching out the property lines, she began drawing loose circles within its boundaries to organize the space into functional areas. "This part of the yard may be best

"*Through rounds of revisions, the shape and size of the spiral changed, the bench was integrated into a low stone wall, and a small fountain was added at the center.*"

for the children's play area," she said, "because you can see it from both the kitchen and the family room. They need a patio for entertaining just outside the back door. We want the hot tub near the master bedroom. And the meditation garden belongs at the rear of the property, where it's quiet and secluded." And on she went, melding the client's wish list with what she knew about the space.

A bubble diagram is much like the outline I create before writing a story. It's the big picture, the key points, a way to organize all the random thoughts and ideas into a meaningful working structure. This bubble diagram, later refined on drafting paper, would become the basis for designing a concept plan, also sometimes called a master plan.

LET THE IDEAS FLOW, EVEN IF THEY'RE ROUGH

As a writer, I like to look for anecdotes, analogies, or interesting ideas to kick off the writing process. It's a good way to overcome writer's block. Apparently, the same approach works for designers. The Suchards' idea for a spiral meditation garden intrigued Jeni and had the potential to become the focal point of the garden. So that's where she started—exploring related symbolism, making lists of healing plants, and thinking about how a meditative space should feel.

Jeni began sketching a grassy spiral path (the spiral is an often-used symbol for self-exploration and inner growth) through an herb garden, leading to a central bench for meditation. Through rounds of revisions, the shape and size of the spiral changed, the bench was integrated into a low stone wall, and a small fountain was added at the center. As the plans developed, this garden would become the primary view from the family room, and would serve to anchor the backyard.

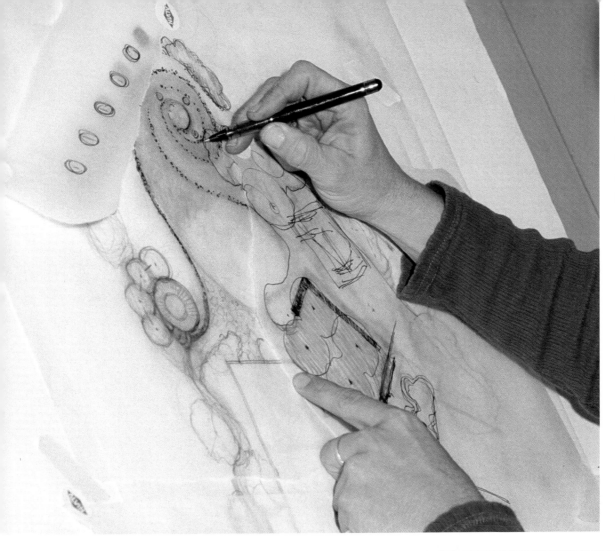

Using tissue overlays is similar to writing rough drafts. Several different approaches to an area can be tested without redrawing the entire plan.

Section Drawings Offer Dimensional Views

Sometimes it helps to draw a section view instead of an overhead view. This sketch of cypress trees and shrubs better illustrates what you'd see looking toward the back property line.

A Geometric Grid Places Elements in Alignment

By projecting the lines of the house to the property boundaries, and designing within grids, landscape elements were placed in proper relation to one another and to the house.

Once her creative juices were flowing, Jeni moved on to more practical matters. "Early in the process, you need to deal with your systems—pathways, terrain and drainage issues, hardscaped areas, and major planting areas. You also need to think about your sight lines, both from within the house and from critical points in the yard."

With that in mind, she started sketching paths to connect the house and garage and to wrap around the house. She designed a patio, changing its shape and size a number of times, added some pollarded sycamores for shade, and connected the patio to a vine-covered arbor. She then sketched in the play area, drew a hot tub surrounded by a tiny forest, sited fast-growing trees for screening the view of neighboring houses, and removed a few rails from the front porch to provide better access to the driveway.

As she worked, Jeni kept asking the question "What if?" out loud, as if I were expected to answer. "What if I changed the shape of the patio? What if I designed a low wall to double as seating? What if I went with a more natural approach instead of a geometric design out front?" She later explained that "What if?" is the most important question a designer can ask. "It gives you new ways of thinking."

As I watched Jeni work and rework each segment of the plan, I was reminded of working on my own rough drafts, beginnings of ideas that are either tossed or retooled. Jeni went through her share of tissue paper, creating dozens of overlays that could be taped onto the site plan, each with a different idea or approach. She worked mostly in pencil, frequently picking up an eraser to make changes.

CREATE A SENSE OF PLACE

Just like a story, a garden needs a setting. Jeni believes it's important to create a sense of place, to tie the garden to the vernacular landscape. "If you want a tropical garden or English border, that's fine, but mix in some indigenous hardscaping materials, add some familiar architectural details, and integrate at least a few native plants into the design."

She also believes in sharing gardens with wildlife. "New housing has eliminated so much of the natural habitat for birds and animals that anything we can do to provide them with food, water, and shelter is worthwhile."

Whenever possible, she tries to maintain a distant view, whether natural or man-made. "You experience a better sense of well-being if you have a view; otherwise, you tend to feel closed in." Borrowed views are fine. At the Suchards', they have a view of trees on neighboring land, so Jeni will leave that side of the property open, rather than planting a screen.

Once she had the general spaces laid out, Jeni began working on the details, keeping the Suchards' home, the local architecture, and the Napa Valley vegetation in mind. She selected stone for the patio that complemented the foundation of the house, covered the arbor with grapevines, chose cypress trees for screening the view of nearby rooftops, called for a mature olive tree to anchor the front yard, and designed a dense hedge of native oaks along the creek. Because silver is a predominant vegetation color in the region (as seen in sages, olives, and oaks), she included lots of silver-foliaged herbs in the meditation garden.

DON'T FORGET THE PEOPLE

When you're isolated in a studio, it's easy to get carried away with the creative process. But Jeni didn't let this happen. As she pointed out, "You can't forget the people." And this plan really was about the homeowners. It considered how each family member would use the space. The kids had a place to swing and play, as well as pathways for riding their bikes; Jody had a small vegetable and flower garden to

> ## "Designing to satisfy everyone in a household is a tall order."

putter around in; and David had his trees. There was a patio for entertaining and a redesigned front yard to welcome frequent guests. And traffic patterns had been improved so that it was easier to get from the house to the car, and to take out the trash at the end of the day.

Designing to satisfy everyone in a household is a tall order. As Jeni says, "You can't just look for compromises that everyone can live with or you'll be designing to the lowest common denominator. You have to negotiate, so that everyone gets something special. And sometimes, you have to realize that emotions and attachments are even more important than aesthetics."

GEOMETRY REFINES A PLAN

Since our goal was to complete this plan during my visit, Jeni and I spent some late nights together in the studio. On the last night, I sensed some frustration. The front yard had been reworked a dozen times—first with climbing roses and then with standard roses; with raised beds and without; with the vegetable garden front center, and later moved to a less prominent position near the front-porch railing. Out back, both the patio and spiral garden looked great—but they didn't quite work together. It was midnight, and I crossed the line, making my first suggestion: "Why don't we call it a day. You can look at it fresh in the morning." An hour and a half later, she finally agreed.

The truth is, Jeni didn't even know what time it was. That sometimes happens when you're immersed in a project. Even so, it's amaz-

Sacred Geometry Is Used to Design the Meditation Garden

The meditation garden was based on the shape of a nautilus, or spiral—one of the perfect geometric shapes found in nature. Its dimensions are derived from a series of squares created with a rectangle (see overlay).

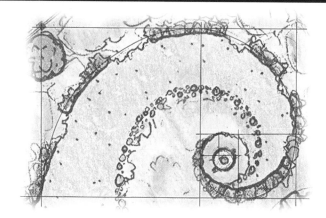

ing what a good night's sleep will do. The next morning, I headed off for a photo shoot while Jeni returned to the studio. When I caught up with her mid-morning, the plans on her drawing table looked quite different. The many layers of tissue were gone, and in their place was a single sheet of drafting paper with a nice, neat plan. The previous night's problems had been resolved, and a few new ideas had been included. The changes were subtle, but significant.

When I asked what had happened, Jeni launched into a discussion about geometry. "You have to think of landscape elements in relation to the house. Square everything off and work within a grid," she said, rather matter-of-factly. In explaining this further, she described how she had extended the lines of the house to the property boundary and reworked each of the landscape features to fit along or within the lines of the grid. This resulted in changing the size and angle of the patio, shifting the hot tub over a few feet, and simplifying the bed lines in the front yard.

Jeni also used a bit of sacred geometry, which is based on perfect geometric shapes that are found in nature. The meditation garden was designed as a spiral or paisley, which is derived from the shape of a nautilus.

The geometric overlay tied together all the individual elements of the plan, putting them in correct relation to one another and to the house. It's sort of like having a consistent theme run throughout a story you're writing.

AND FINALLY, A CONCEPT PLAN

The finishing touches were placed on the plan, and blueprints were made by running the original through the duplicating machine. A final drawing was colored with pencils for presentation to the clients, who, by the way, were pleased with the results. Prior to installation, Jeni will add any client changes to the plan, create detailed planting plans, and draw construction details for some of the hardscaping and irrigation projects.

Jeni had some final words about the creative process for me before I caught my flight back to Connecticut: "Remember, a concept plan is just that—a concept. Once you start installing a garden, you tend to tweak a plan as you see it taking shape. It's just your initial vision; it shouldn't restrict what you do with your site." And with that, I headed for the airport, eager to get started not only on my story but on some new ideas for my garden.

A Concept Plan

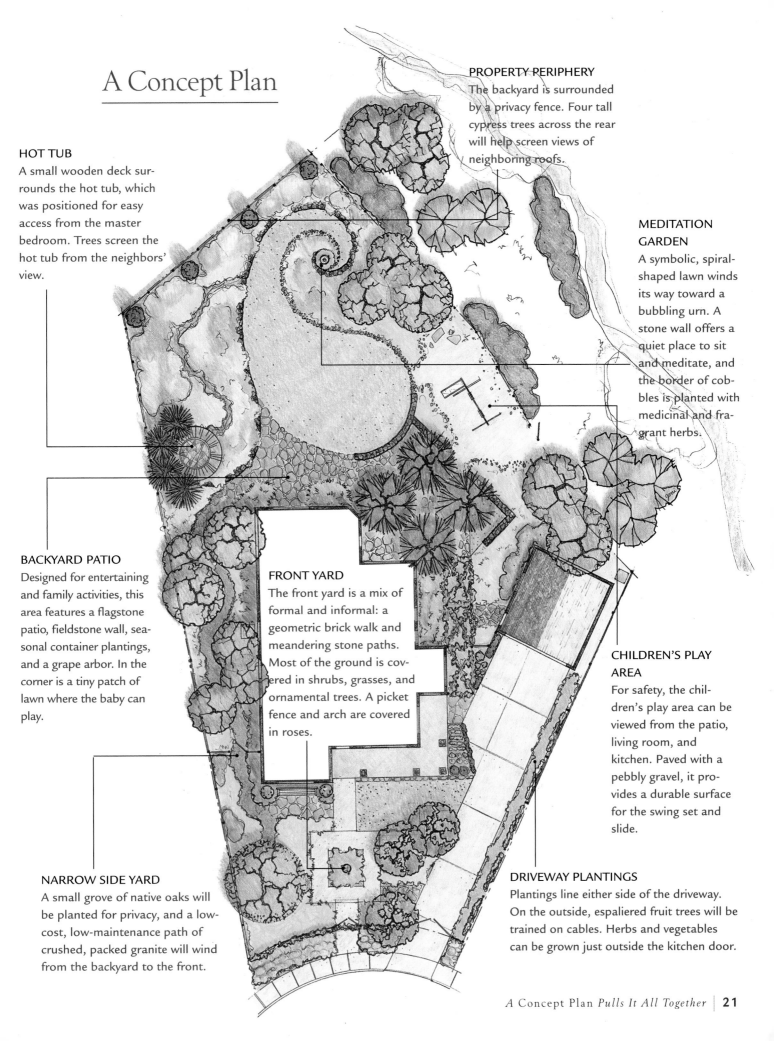

HOT TUB
A small wooden deck surrounds the hot tub, which was positioned for easy access from the master bedroom. Trees screen the hot tub from the neighbors' view.

PROPERTY PERIPHERY
The backyard is surrounded by a privacy fence. Four tall cypress trees across the rear will help screen views of neighboring roofs.

MEDITATION GARDEN
A symbolic, spiral-shaped lawn winds its way toward a bubbling urn. A stone wall offers a quiet place to sit and meditate, and the border of cobbles is planted with medicinal and fragrant herbs.

BACKYARD PATIO
Designed for entertaining and family activities, this area features a flagstone patio, fieldstone wall, seasonal container plantings, and a grape arbor. In the corner is a tiny patch of lawn where the baby can play.

FRONT YARD
The front yard is a mix of formal and informal: a geometric brick walk and meandering stone paths. Most of the ground is covered in shrubs, grasses, and ornamental trees. A picket fence and arch are covered in roses.

CHILDREN'S PLAY AREA
For safety, the children's play area can be viewed from the patio, living room, and kitchen. Paved with a pebbly gravel, it provides a durable surface for the swing set and slide.

NARROW SIDE YARD
A small grove of native oaks will be planted for privacy, and a low-cost, low-maintenance path of crushed, packed granite will wind from the backyard to the front.

DRIVEWAY PLANTINGS
Plantings line either side of the driveway. On the outside, espaliered fruit trees will be trained on cables. Herbs and vegetables can be grown just outside the kitchen door.

1 COLOR

Complementary and contrasting colors. Tints, hues, and tones. Primaries and pastels. They're all part of the color equation. Jazz it up or stick with soothing tones. In the end, it's all a matter of personal taste.

2 TEXTURE

Smooth, rough, soft, prickly, glossy, or fuzzy. Go for contrast—mixing the delicate with the bold, the soft with the rough. Foliage, flowers, bark, and hardscaping materials all have texture.

5 TOUCH

From the fuzzy foliage of lamb's ears to the ticklish fronds of ornamental grasses, plants are meant to be touched, even caressed. Don't forget the feel of aged wood, polished pebbles, and other nonplant materials.

6 FUNCTION

How should your space be used? For a child's play area? To grow vegetables? For meditation? Or outdoor entertaining? Design areas with a purpose. Don't forget practical matters, like the trash and compost pile.

7 LIGHT

Take note of the patterns of light and shadow in your garden. Backlight translucent flowers and let grassy plumes shimmer in the evening light. Build an arbor to create a shady spot for hot summer days.

11 PERSPECTIVE

How will you view your garden? From a deck, through a window, at ground level? Will you see the garden all at once or discover small sections as you move about? Perspective changes the way a garden is experienced.

12 MOTION

Water running through a stream bed. Butterflies dancing over flower heads. Tall grasses swaying in the wind. Birds flitting from tree to tree. Motion gives life to a garden.

3 SCENT

What could be better than the sweet scent of a jasmine, daphne, rose, rosemary, or lilac? Plant something fragrant near your window and outdoor seating areas. And grow something fragrant for every season.

4 SOUND

The trickling of a stream, the splash of a fountain, the chirping of birds, the rustling of leaves, or the soft melody of chimes can soothe the soul and drown out distractions.

8 PATTERN

Knot gardens, boxwood parterres, brick paving, picket fences—they all create pattern in the garden. Take your time and strive for perfection. Minor details make or break patterns.

9 FORM

Think three-dimensional, and go for variety. Plants may be rounded, columnar, spreading, upright, billowing, or fountainlike. Hardscaping materials and garden ornaments have form too.

10 CONTRAST

Contrast attracts attention and pleases the eye. Just a bit of contrast is soothing. A lot of contrast is stimulating. You can contrast color, texture, form, and light.

13 MOVEMENT

How will you move through the garden? Will you meander along curving paths, or get where you're going in a more businesslike fashion with straight paths? This is a situation where form follows function.

14 CHANGE

Trees grow tall, creating shade where there once was sun. Perennials spread to outgrow their spaces. Soft morning light changes to harsh noonday sun. Flowers turn to seedheads. Welcome change to your garden. Plan for it.

15 ASPECT

Dust off your compass and find true north. How will you position your house and gardens? Remember that what's shady in one season may be bright and sunny in another. It's all a matter of personal taste.

16 PERSONALITY

Old-fashioned flowers. Whirly-gigs and gazing globes. A formal Italian folly. Architectural antiques. Or soothing garden sculptures. What has special meaning to you? Let people know this is your garden.

17 FOCAL POINTS

Whether it's a waterfall at the end of a path, a Japanese maple in a mixed border, or a nicely plant-ed pot at your door, create a special place for the eye to rest. Use focal points judiciously—too many will just create confusion.

18 ECOLOGY

Invite wildlife to your garden. Grow some native plants. Opt for sustainably harvested and recycled materials when possible, and use only as much hardscaping as you really need.

19 SENSE OF PLACE

Let your garden echo the vernacular landscape. Mix in some native plants or local stone. Weave in colloquial expression. And add your own personality, creating a garden that is uniquely yours.

20 ARCHITECTURE

Echo your home's architecture in the garden. Repeat motifs, shapes, colors, patterns, and building materials. Bring architecture to the garden—through patios, decks, arbors, gazebos, fences, and more.

JENI WEBBER

is a residential landscape architect in Oakland, California. She has been designing gardens for more than 15 years.

Draw *Your Own* Site Plan

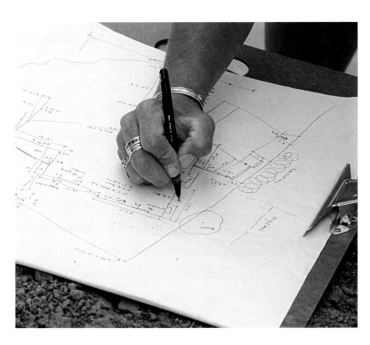

Make a rough, working sketch of your home and property. Don't worry if it's not to scale; you just need a place to write down all of your measurements.

I LEARNED TO DRAW landscape plans in graduate school. Even so, I never got around to drawing one for my mother's garden, which served as my garden laboratory. That's why I had to move the apple tree three times and remove a rose bed for which I hadn't negotiated rights. If I had taken the time to draw a plan, I would have known the apple tree wouldn't receive enough light where I planted it and that it would ruin a view of the garden. And had I shared this plan with my mother, she would have let me know that she cherished her lush lawn, and didn't want to give it up for a rose garden, no matter how beautiful the flowers.

True, creating a plan takes a little effort. But a plan allows you to play around with ideas and change your mind without pulling out the shovel—to go from wildly impractical dreams to workable solutions before you dig the first hole. A plan is especially helpful when there are two or more interested parties, as you can more amicably work out

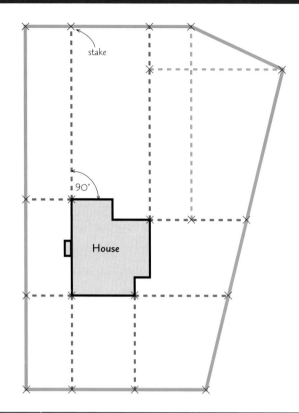

Establishing Property Boundaries

stake

90°

House

1 Measure the distance from any four corners of your house to the property line. To do this accurately, square yourself up with the house by looking straight down a wall (blue).

2 Measure each leg of the property line, from corner to corner and between all corners and stakes (green).

3 If you have an odd angle, take additional measurements (orange) squared off from your original line running from the house to the stakes (blue). While not essential, this measurement makes it easier to identify the angles when you sit down at the drawing board.

Start with everything. Even the location of seemingly unimportant items like hose bibs can play into your final design.

solutions to your differing needs and desires. A plan lets you place plants thoughtfully—keeping in mind how large they'll grow over time. And I find I can think about seasonal changes more easily when I work on paper. In fact, as far as I'm concerned, a plan is almost as essential as a shovel when you're landscaping.

But before you play with design ideas on paper, you need to draw an accurate site plan, or base map. It will include the property boundaries, house, driveway, paths, outbuildings, trees, and other existing features or plantings. Once you have this site plan, you can use tissue-paper overlays to play around with new design ideas for your property.

MAKE A ROUGH SKETCH

Site plans aren't difficult to draw, but you do need to obtain accurate measurements. And because not all of the features on your proper-

ty fall along straight lines, it helps to know a few tricks for obtaining these measurements.

First, gather your materials together. You need a pen, a large sheet of paper (approximately 18 by 24 inches), an oversized artist's clipboard, about a dozen stakes, and both 100-foot and 25-foot tape measures. A plat (often referred to as a survey) from your city or town hall is a bonus, but is not necessary; you would want to double-check it for accuracy anyway. If measuring grade changes is important—for instance, if you want to build a retaining wall or steps—you'll also need string, and a string level (available at any hardware store), and more stakes.

First, roughly sketch your property boundaries and house on your paper. Don't worry about drawing to scale. This sketch serves as a point of reference for making notes and jotting down measurements. By creating a rough

Measure a Curved Bed or Border

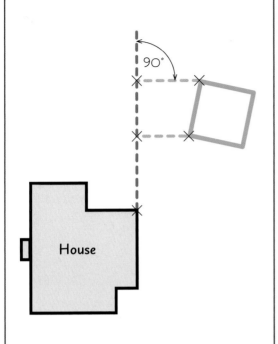

1 Once again, establish squared-off lines from appropriate corners of the house. Mark 5- or 10-foot increments down this line (blue).

2 Measure the perpendicular distance from your marks to the edge of the border (orange). When you draw the bed, simply connect the dots.

---

doors and windows is important so that you can design your entries and views from the house. And by measuring both the overall length and width of the house in addition to the individual elements, you can double-check your measurements.

Be sure to note the location of downspouts, hose-bibs, air-conditioners, and meter boxes and indicate any roof overhang. These elements will be important to your final design. Write these measurements on your sketch using any method of shorthand that you can later interpret. Work your way around the house until you have returned to your starting point. Chances are, you'll have a few more twigs and leaves in your hair than when you started, but you'll also have the measurements you need to draw your house to scale when you sit down at the drawing table.

NEXT MEASURE YOUR PROPERTY

Once you finish measuring the house, move on to the property boundaries. First, measure the distance from our house to the property lines. Starting at that same corner of your house, walk to the edge of your property.

Where's north? Use a compass to determine the positioning of your property and aspect of your home.

---

sketch before you begin, you won't run out of space on the paper halfway through the project.

FIRST MEASURE YOUR HOUSE

Start at any corner of your house, which hopefully is not in the middle of a prickly bush. Run your 100-foot tape measure the length of the house for an overall measurement, and then measure the individual elements. For example, you might find that the overall length is 54 feet; that there is a 3-foot-wide window 5 feet from the corner; and that at 27 feet, a 6-foot front-porch landing extends 4 feet from the house. Noting the location of

Placing Trees or Shrubs

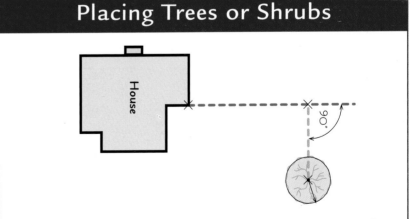

1 Establish a squared-off line from any corner of your house to the pro perty line (blue). Measure the distance from the house to a point on the line perpendicular to the tree.

2 Then measure the distance from the point to the tree (orange). The lines must be at right angles to each other.

Measuring grade is easy. Just stretch a string between two stakes (one at the top of the grade and one a lower point), level it off with a string level, and then measure the distance from the string to the ground.

When you reach the boundary, turn around and square yourself up with the house—moving sideways until you can see straight down the length of a wall. Mark this spot with a stake (as you'll refer to it later) and note the distance from the stake to the house on your sketch. Repeat this process, from the same corner, but in the direction perpendicular to the side you just measured. Then repeat it again, measuring the distance to the property lines from all four corners of your house. (If your house isn't a simple rectangle, just select any four corners for reference.) Don't assume that the distance to the property line is the same from any two corners. Even a difference of a few feet can have a significant effect on your design, especially with features like decks and patios. To finish with your property boundaries, measure the overall lengths of the property lines as well as the distances between corners and stakes along the lines.

MEASURE PERMANENT FEATURES AND PLANTINGS

Once you are comfortable with the relationship between the house and the property boundaries, it's time to include driveways, paths, patios, and outbuildings. Again, it helps to start with a rough sketch of these elements (on the same sheet of paper) before you take the measurements.

First, measure the distances from the property corners to where the driveway and any paths or fences cross the property lines. Second, measure outbuildings and terraces in relation to the house. Measure distances to corners from known points (such as your house, the property line, or the measuring line that runs from your house to the property line); and then measure their dimensions, as you measured around the house.

The next items to include on the base plan are any existing trees and planting beds. The easiest way that I know to do this is by running a long tape measure from the corner of the house to the property boundary where you placed a stake, and then, with your short tape measure, calculating the distance that your subject is from a point on the tape measure (illustration, p. 27). For instance, 25 feet out and 4 feet to the right of the northeast corner is an oak tree with a spread of 20 feet. A similar approach works for curved beds, except that you take a series of measurements approximately every 10 feet (illustration, p. 27).

HOW TO MEASURE GRADE

For most home landscaping projects, you won't need to measure the grade. However, it is valuable to obtain grade changes if you want to install terracing or retaining walls. It is also important for calculating rise, run, and number of steps. Calculating grade is not necessary if you are simply planting a hillside.

While there are several ways to measure grade, the easiest calls for a string level. To get an overall feel for the slope of your land, start at the top of the grade and pound a short stake into the ground. Hook your short tape measure to the stake, walk down the hill (5 to 10 feet for steep grades and 15 to 20 feet for gradual grades), and mark that spot with a tall stake. Tie the string to the bottom of your short stake and stretch it out to your tall stake. Hang the level on the string, and pull the string taut. When the bubble is in the center of the level, tie the string to your tall stake and measure the distance from the string to the ground. This will tell you how many feet your property drops in the distance you measured. To measure a long slope, simply repeat this process, using your tall stake as your starting point, and working your way down the hill.

If you already know where you want to place your retaining wall or steps, follow the same procedure, but measure the distance from the top of your steps or wall to the bottom.

MAKE A SCALE DRAWING

Once you've gathered your measurements, you are ready to tackle the next step in creating a site plan—laying it out on paper in it's final form. Find a flat surface where you can remain set up for a few hours, and gather your supplies. You will need 20 by 30-inch vellum paper (plain or gridded), masking tape, pencils, an eraser, a T-square, and at least one drafting triangle (either 30- or 45-degrees, with a right angle and sides at least 6 inches long). You will also need a three-sided architect's ruler, which converts your measurements to scale. I recommend the vellum paper because you can run blueprint copies of your sketches; finding a photocopy machine to make duplicates of a large sketch is difficult. All items can be picked up at an art supply store.

To determine your working scale, divide the length of your property by the working length of the paper. For instance, to draw a 100-foot-long property line in a 25-inch space (this leaves a bit of white space around the edge of your 30-inch paper), you'll work in ¼-inch scale, or 1 inch for every 4 feet. Use the largest scale that still fits on the paper. If you come up with an odd fraction, simple round it off to ¹⁄₁₀, ⅛, ¼, or ½ scale. I work at ¼-scale for most landscape plans.

Start by lightly drawing the property boundaries on your paper. It doesn't have to be exact, as you are just trying to center your sketch at this point. Now estimate the location of your house in relation to the property

boundary. Lightly mark the overall dimensions of your house, adjusting the paper to line up one side with the T-square (which will let you use your triangles to square everything off). Then go back and draw the house to scale, noting your detailed measurements. Next, measuring from the house, systematically place the landscape on the paper, starting with the house and property lines (which may vary slightly from that first light sketch you made), then moving to the other landscape elements.

Double check your measurements and evaluate the developing plan to make sure that it looks right. If you have any problems making things work out, simply go outside and re-measure the tricky spot. And finally, pull out your compass, find north, and put this on your sketcth. Once you've completed your site plan, give yourself a pat on the back and go for an inspirational walk before you start playing around with new ideas for your landscape.

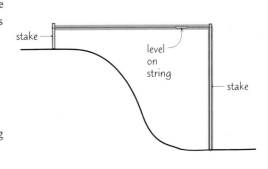

Measuring an Outbuilding or Terrace

1 Establish a squared-off line from the nearest house corner (blue).

2 Measure the distance from two points on this line out to two corners of your outbuilding or terrace (orange). The lines much be at right angles to each other.

3 Measure the building or terrace (green).

Design Your Own
Planting Plan

C. COLSTON BURRELL

is a garden designer, author, photographer, and naturalist. He is principal of Native Landscape Design and Restoration, a firm that blends nature and culture through artistic design.

With a planting plan, you can experiment with ideas on paper before spending money on plants or digging any holes.

BEFORE I DESIGN a garden, I indulge in dreaming. I put my trowel aside and stay away from nurseries until I have a sense of what I'd like to see take shape. Only then do I narrow my focus and get down to nuts and bolts.

Turning a dream of a garden into reality requires some type of plan or design. And, designing a garden is easier than you think, if you follow some tried-and-true steps. Basically, putting plans on paper is a way to visualize and express ideas in a concrete format.

Mastering a few simple skills will let you communicate ideas on paper and draw on logic and intuition. It's important to remember that the design process doesn't move neatly from one point to another. During design stages we play with possibilities, respond to what's on paper, and clarify our visions. Taking the time to draw plans will help any gardener become more adept at arranging plants in ways that seem balanced, unified, rhythmical, and dynamic.

31

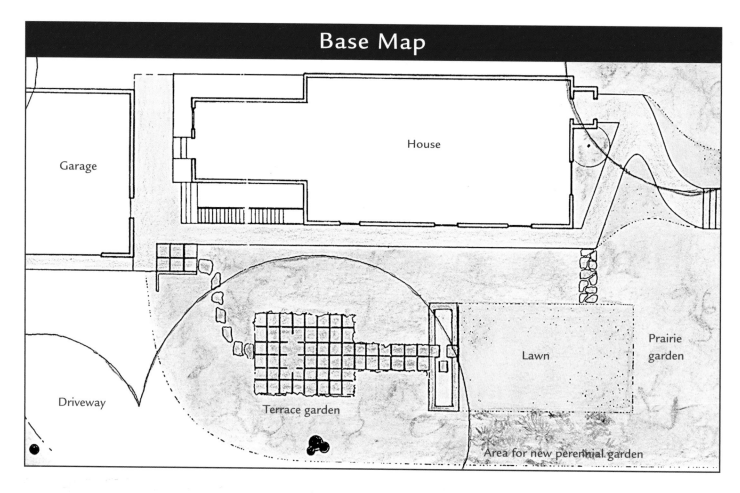

Garage

House

Driveway

Terrace garden

Lawn

Prairie garden

Area for new perennial garden

START WITH A BASE MAP OF YOUR SITE

It's useful to have a base map of your site as a planning tool before you design a garden. You can use this map to chart sun-and-shade patterns and see how the proposed garden relates to the rest of the site. You may be able to get a working site map or survey from the title company that handled the sale of the property or your local planning and zoning board.

If you can't get your hands on a map, draw one. First, measure the yard, including the proposed garden area. Indicate the corners of the house and property lines as reference points. Then measure any features in the yard that will be within or next to the garden, such as sidewalks, outbuildings, and trees.

Back inside, tape a large sheet of graph paper to a table, using a T square to position the page squarely. Represent the site's dimensions on the graph paper. It's common to have one square on the graph paper equal 1 to 2 ft. of actual length. If you're creating a large garden, one square per 3 ft. may work better. Use the T square and a triangle to square the edges of the property lines and the house, and to draw linear areas such as driveways and walks. Use a template to draw small circles representing tree trunks, and large circles to show tree canopies. Don't try to make this map a work of art. It's simply a planning tool that will be useful for all your garden-making efforts.

"It's important to remember that design is not a process that moves neatly from one point to another.

ASSESS SUN-AND-SHADE PATTERNS

Make three copies of your map to record sun-and-shade patterns. Pick a sunny day in late spring or early summer, after the trees have leafed out. Using separate copies of the map for different times, color in areas that are in shade at 10 a.m., at 1 p.m., and at 4 p.m. You can also use this information to make tracing-paper overlays, and combine them to show which areas get the most and least sun. These studies will help you place your garden beds and choose plants accordingly. You may be surprised to find that some areas get more sun than you thought, and others less.

LOCATION, LOCATION, LOCATION

Where you place the garden determines what you can grow. Conversely, what you want to

"Where you place the garden determines what you can grow."

grow may influence where you place the garden. Review your sun-and-shade study to choose the most appropriate location. If you're set on a particular spot, the maps will guide you in plant selection. If the spot is shadier or sunnier than you wanted, reevaluate your site and plant choices. Also address factors such as traffic patterns and the garden's proximity to water spigots.

Next, consider the size of your planned garden in practical and aesthetic terms. For a perennial garden, you need ample space for a variety of plants to have a full season of blooms. Aim to include at least 30 to

Section Drawing for Perennial Garden

Planting Plan for Perennial Garden

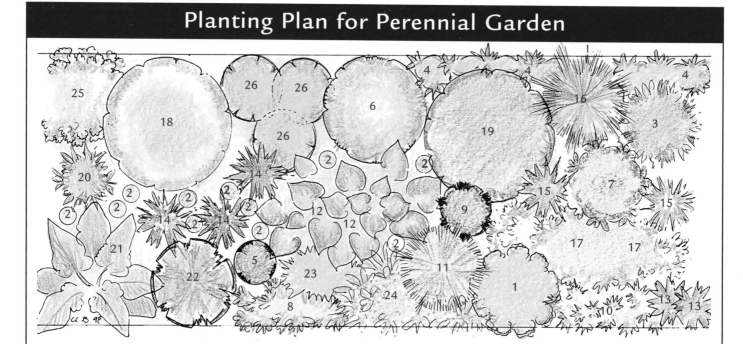

KEY:

1 Lady's mantle
2 Stars of Persia
3 Willow blue star
4 'Honorine Jobert' Japanese anemone
5 'Ada Ballard' aster
6 Goatsbeard

7 Blue false indigo
8 Biokovo' Cambridge geranium
9 Caucasus geranium
10 Lancaster geranium
11 Blue oat grass
12 Royal Standard' hosta
13 Dwarf bearded iris

14 'Orville Fay' Siberian iris
15 'White Swirl' Siberian iris
16 Purple silver grass
17 Blue Wonder' catmint
18 'Lotus Queen' peony
19 'Sea Shell' peony
20 'Husker Red' penstemon

21 Rhubarb
22 'May Night' sage
23 'Golden Fleece' goldenrod
24 Lamb's ear
25 Yellow meadow rue
26 Carolina lupine

40 plants. If possible, make room for small trees and shrubs, as well as perennials, annuals, and bulbs. Avoid creating small, unrelated planting areas.

To accommodate graduated layering of plants, beds should be at least 3 to 4 ft. deep. Linear beds with two-sided access can be 5 to 6 ft. deep without a central path or stepping stones, since the average person can reach into a bed about 2½ to 3 ft. For maintenance purposes, a one-sided border without rear access should not be deeper than 3 ft. When beds are 6 to 8 ft. deep, you can create a backdrop of low-care flowering shrubs, with flowers in front. Longer beds allow room to repeat unifying colors and forms.

Keep in mind that the farther away the garden is from viewing points, the larger it must be to make an impact. A good starting size for a border is 8 ft. wide by 24 ft. long, but choose a size to fit your location, as well as time and budget constraints. When in doubt, start small.

PLAY WITH GARDEN SHAPES ON PAPER

Armed with your sun-and-shade drawings and an idea of the garden's ultimate size, you can begin drafting. Draw your ideas for the size and shape of the garden on tracing paper overlaid on the base map. Play with different shapes and save each version for reflection.

When you draw one that really excites you, evaluate the practical aspects of the design. Is the bed narrow enough for you to reach to the center from either side? If not, how will you get into it? You may need stepping stones or a central path in order to do maintenance. How will the shape of your lawn be affected? You don't want to end up with a misshapen panel of turf that's impossible to mow. The bed must fit with the overall design of your yard, and relate comfortably to the house.

When you settle on a pleasing size and shape, use a garden hose to lay out the bed in the yard. If it looks right, transfer the lines to a copy of your original base map, or create a new map of just the garden area on a larger scale, with perhaps 3 squares equaling 1 foot. Make copies of this new working map for design experiments, or use tracing paper to make overlays.

MAKE A PLANT CHART AND SECTION DRAWING

Choosing plants is the fun part of garden design. Start by making a list of all the plants you want to grow and make sure that they'll thrive under your soil, moisture, and light conditions. Then, make a chart with the names of these plants, with columns for the color, bloom time, height, and spread of every plant. Once completed, this chart becomes a valuable design tool.

Now you're ready to begin designing your bed. Lay a piece of tracing paper over your garden map and use the actual length of the bed as the parameter. Since I'm familiar with plant characteristics and used to drawing, I draft my preliminary designs in a two-dimensional profile drawing first. This drawing is called a section. I draw plants roughly to scale, but I'm not slavish to dimensions at this point. I represent plants as they will look in the design—mounded, spiky, flat, and such.

I design beds and borders by using key plants as the basis for creating combinations with other plants. Then I link all these plant groupings to create a unified design. Review your chart and choose a few outstanding plants that bloom in different seasons. Use these as anchors in your design and build combinations by surrounding them with complementary plants that bloom at the same time. This will strengthen the visual appeal of your garden.

If you're not comfortable drawing plant shapes, you can use cutouts of plants to visualize how plant forms, textures, and colors work together. Clip pictures of plants you have chosen from old nursery catalogs and try different combinations until you get a pleasing design. Then fasten the pictures to their intended place in the design using tape or rubber cement, as you would create a collage. If you don't like a plant's position, peel it off and try it in another spot.

As you combine plants, consider the color and size of the flower, the form of the plant, and foliage texture. I limit color choices to ensure a unified design. In a small garden, too many colors look chaotic, rather than harmonious. Choose a cool or warm color scheme, or create a color harmony. Stick to your choices and resist the temptation to throw in one more favorite plant just because you want to grow it.

Contrast billowing, airy plants with bold-textured plants. Place rounded forms next to spiky forms and use low-mounding or trailing plants at the front of the border to unify the

"The farther away the garden is from viewing points, the larger it must be to make an impact."

edge. Placing too many similar shapes together results in dull combinations. The tallest plants work best toward the middle or back of the border, although tall, see-through plants like *Verbena bonariensis* may be pulled forward. Include enough variety to keep it interesting. Style and taste are personal, so there are no right or wrong combinations.

Link individual plant combinations together with species that will unify the design through repetition of color, form, or texture. These unifying elements are essential to make the garden look and feel right. Bridge pleasing, varied combinations until you have filled out the bed.

It pays to do enough research at this stage so that your design will work from season to sea-son. Knowing the characteristics of plants means you can layer them to get the most impact in the smallest space. For example, you can have a spring-flowering combination that is followed by new combinations of blooms in summer and again in fall. You can use one plant to show off another or to fill a space left when one goes dormant. Make each plant pay its rent.

PUT YOUR PLANTING PLAN ON PAPER

After you draw the garden in section, or make a collage of cutouts, you need to convert it to a planting plan—representing plants as circles or shapes viewed from above. Refer to your chart for the spread of the plants. Use a circle tem-

&

"I design beds and borders by using key plants as the basis for creating combinations with other plants."

plate and ruler to determine which circle matches the plants' mature sizes by measuring the diameter of the circle and converting it to the scale of your drawing. This will vary depending on the scale of your map. You can also use the squares on the graph paper as a guide. Represent the plants with a series of circles or shapes that are arranged on paper as they will be in the garden. Let the edges overlap, since plants will interweave in the garden. I like the garden to be full, without gaps between plants, so I space them close together.

Once you record the combinations on paper, you can test the design by drawing colored-pencil overlays over the planting plan. Using your plant chart as a reference, make four different overlays—one for spring, early summer, late summer, and autumn. Place a piece of tracing paper over the design and show the colors of plants in bloom during each season. Remember that all sections of the garden can't be in bloom at once, but make sure you have pleasing color combinations and ample blooms during each season.

When your design is done, calculate how many plants you need to buy. Since your plan is to scale, it will be easy to figure. Give each different plant a number in your chart, and use those numbers as the key to your design. Place the appropriate number in each circle or shape and then count the numbers representing each plant.

PLANT YOUR GARDEN USING A GRID

Take your plan and a tape measure when you lay out the bed. Use wooden stakes and string to indicate the garden's shape. Prepare the planting bed by completely removing unwanted turf, amending the soil, and raking the surface smooth.

"You can test the design by drawing colored-pencil overlays over the planting plan."

When you're ready to plant, use the tape measure, stakes, and string to mark off the horizontal lines of your grid. Pick 1-, 2- or 3-foot grid intervals, depending on the size of the garden and the intricacy of the design. A small grid works best for intricate combinations. Use additional stakes and string to mark off the width of the bed. Mark off the entire grid.

Another option is to use biosafe florist's paint to outline the grid. First, measure the grid squares as described above, but trace the lines of the grid in the soil using a rake handle or other instrument. Then spray the lines on the soil with the paint.

Now you can plant according to the plan, relying on the grid to get the spacing right. Measure the length of your trowel and use it like a ruler to fine tune within the grid. I prefer to lay out the plants in their respective places before I plant. After I see the combinations in place, I adjust the design as necessary.

TWEAK THE DESIGN AS IT MATURES

A garden is a work in progress throughout the gardener's life. Whether it's three months or three years old, there's always need for fine tuning. Don't be afraid to move plants around as they grow or even to revamp your whole garden. And, if you want to update the key to your garden, use copies of the planting plan with tracing-paper overlays to indicate new locations of plants.

Laura and Jay Perry reflect on the changes they've made in the garden. It has taken five years to transform their open lot into a series of intimate, functional garden rooms.

LAURA E. PERRY

is an avid gardener in Baltimore, Maryland. She collaborated with landscape architect Catherine Mahan of Mahan Rykiel Associates, Inc. on the development of these gardens.

Working
from a Master
Plan

I HAD BEEN A PASSIONATE amateur gardener for years before Jay and I became engaged, but the property surrounding his—soon to be our—house in Baltimore presented some daunting challenges.

The square lot was really two rectangular lots with the house stuck in one corner. A line of unkempt pachysandra and privet served as a reminder of where the lots had once been divided. There was little privacy from neighboring houses, no place to sit outside comfortably, and no real landscaping to enhance the property. The overgrown garden had no shape or design, and several raised beds with roses and daylilies just seemed out of place. How were we to transform this into an area where we could entertain, the children could play, and I could indulge my love for gardening?

My wedding gift to Jay was a professionally designed master plan, created by a landscape architect, that we could implement ourselves as time and money allowed.

A grassy terrace and bluestone patio expand living areas outdoors, creating a place for entertaining family and friends.

With a little patience and work, we could have our dream garden, as well as the pleasure of bringing it to life together as newlyweds.

CHOOSING A LANDSCAPE ARCHITECT

When I began looking for a landscape architect in 1991, I had a head full of beautiful images culled from books and other people's gardens. The difficulty lay in sorting through all the possibilities. The lot was larger than I was used to and in such disarray that I needed a professional to narrow the options and organize the space. I wanted a design that would provide clarity and structure, and curb my tendency toward overplanting. But because I love plants, I wanted garden spaces that I could develop over time.

From my work on the Baltimore Parks Board, I knew a number of local landscape architects. Of these, I especially liked the design style and creativity of Mahan Rykiel

"Your designer should be respectful of what you want and like, yet able to help you define your needs."

Associates. Also, I had met Catherine Mahan and found her to be a good listener and, not to be underestimated, someone with a good sense of humor. Personal compatibility is important for a good working relationship with your landscape architect.

When selecting a landscape architect or designer, start by interviewing firms and getting to know their work. Don't just look at plans of their projects; visit the sites themselves. Find the designer with the right style for you. Request client references, and call them to see if the designer performed the work professionally, on time, and on budget.

Make sure your project will get the attention it deserves. Landscape architects specializing in large, commercial jobs might not place a high priority on your project if you have a small lot and a low budget. Make sure they enjoy handling residential projects, and always meet the designer in person. You should feel comfortable with them. After all, you'll be spending a lot of time together. Your designer should be respectful of what you want and like, yet able to help you define your needs.

BUDGETING OPTIONS

Before meeting with Catherine Mahan and her associate, Lydia Kimball, Jay and I discussed our budget. We had two options. We could settle for a design we could afford to build all at once, to plant and enjoy immediately, or we could ask for a more idealistic garden that we would implement ourselves as time and money allowed. We opted for the second approach, reasoning that at the design stage, it doesn't cost any more to think big. I wanted to be sure we didn't pass up a golden design idea just because we couldn't afford to implement it right away.

For many, the first option is unquestionably better. It offers both sensible limits and prompt rewards. Just make sure you don't scrimp on the design itself. Buy the best you can afford. Don't do as I once did and hire a landscape designer for just a few hours; give professionals the time they need to develop the right design for you. After all, you'll be spending good money to bring this vision to life and living with the results for a long time.

The cost of a master plan varies tremendously, depending upon the area you live in, the designer you hire, the size of your property, and the plan's complexity. You could spend as little as $500 to design a small garden or one component of a garden, but easily invest $15,000 for a more comprehensive plan for a large space. Other factors that impact the cost of your plan include how much you use the designer for selecting plants, contracting with vendors, installing hardscapes, and supervising the implementation of the plan.

MAKING A WISH LIST

We let Catherine and Lydia know at the outset that we were engaging them for design only, because we wanted to do most of the legwork ourselves—hiring the contractors, preparing the site, and planting. At our first meeting, the four of us walked around the property together. Catherine and Lydia asked lots of questions about what we liked and didn't like, what we needed, and how the property would be used. Jay and I had already given a great deal of thought to this, and we knew the issues we wanted addressed.

First on our list was the lap pool. We wanted to build it in a place where it wouldn't be visible from the street or obtrusive during the three seasons it would sit idle. The pool should be black and formally shaped, to work as a water feature in the garden when people weren't swimming. And we wanted some shade over or near it.

Adding Rooms to an Open Lot

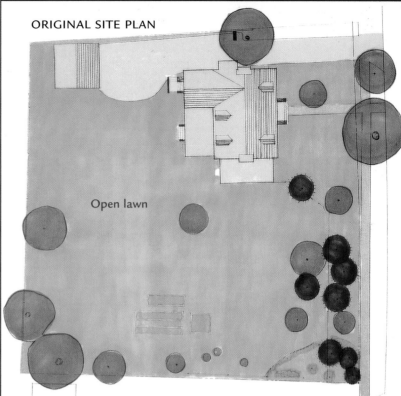

ORIGINAL SITE PLAN

Open lawn

A series of garden rooms transformed an open, double lot (ABOVE) into a more integrated, functional landscape that better relates to the house and family activities (BELOW). Screening was added to establish some privacy.

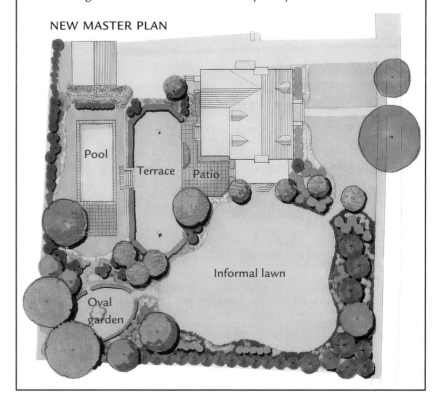

NEW MASTER PLAN

Pool

Terrace   Patio

Informal lawn

Oval garden

DESIGNER VISION AND CLIENT DREAMS MERGE

Our new master plan erased the division between the two lots and created a series of four garden rooms: a formal terrace, a pool area, an informal lawn surrounded by a woodland garden, and a secret, oval garden.

That dividing line of pachysandra and privet was gone, as were the misplaced raised beds and misshapen flower garden. Now our lot was an integrated whole. A stone patio extended the living and entertaining space of the house into the garden. A formal, grassed terrace was bordered by a yew hedge that helped conceal the pool from the street and house. Stone steps led from the terrace to the pool, which, along with its adjoining patio, was placed at the lowest point on the lot. The plan also took full advantage of a beloved pin oak (*Quercus palustris*), using the tree to grace the pool and patio with its dappled shadows.

The children would be able to step off the porch to play on the large, informal lawn, which would be bordered by evergreens and flower beds. Most delightful to me was the oval garden, which Lydia planned as a secret place tucked in a corner of the lot, hidden by a screen of trees and shrubs. Winding stone paths would connect the garden rooms.

Our pre–World War I home is built of fieldstone, with cream-colored wood trim. Above the side porch stands a balcony railing of Chippendale design. Mahan Rykiel copied this design in the new front railing to the porch and subtly applied the theme elsewhere—in the shape of the wide steps off the porch, on the ends of the grassy terrace, and in the little notched bed on the terrace's side.

Although we were pleased with the design, Jay and I did make a few minor revisions. We asked for the area between the patio and the driveway to be paved; this provided easier

The lap pool doubles as a garden feature. The terraced slope and yew hedge help create one of four garden rooms.

We needed an attractive but secure fence to keep neighborhood children away from the pool and our dogs in the yard. Jay's children needed open space to play in, with enough room for baseball and football. To reduce maintenance, we wanted to use trees and shrubs as much as possible. But I also wanted space to grow flowers and thought a cutting garden would be a wonderful luxury.

We wanted space for entertaining outdoors and a way to access the yard and garden from our big side porch. And, because houses in our neighborhood sit quite close together, we desired a little privacy.

Catherine and Lydia also spent time alone in the garden, making notes, taking measurements, and sizing up the space. After that first meeting, Lydia came back and spent several more hours studying the lot. A few weeks later, she unrolled her designs. They took my breath away. She had created a master plan that not only addressed our needs, but greatly enhanced our property.

access for entertaining and moving lawn equipment. We also shifted the pool a few feet farther from the house to prevent children from diving off the terrace wall. Lydia cheerfully complied—the hallmark of a professional. Just as you should be open to your landscape architect's ideas, they should be responsive to your individual needs.

GUIDED BY THE MASTER PLAN

Once the finishing touches were placed on the design, Mahan Rykiel stepped aside, and Jay and I stepped in. As self-proclaimed chief laborer, Jay graded the formal lawn, the oval garden, and the side lawn. I researched and ordered the plants, and we made the final selections together. Our first projects included adding steps from the side porch to the yard, installing the fence, and planting a privacy screen of Leyland cypress (× *cupressocyparis leyandii*). Next, we began dividing up the garden rooms and terracing the slope in the rear of the property. We hired a stonemason to build the wall below the terrace and install the bluestone patio. The stonework proceeded as our budget allowed, taking several years to complete. Two years into the project, we tackled the pool.

Basically, Jay and I have done everything involving dirt: building up the terrace, digging beds out of the lawn, and putting in all the plants. Contractors have done everything involving stone or concrete. Mahan Rykiel recommended qualified contractors for the fence, pool, and tree removal.

Today, we're still adding plants to our garden rooms. We're filling in Mahan Rykiel's design with bushels of color: sunny yellow in the oval garden, pink and blue in the woodland garden, night-friendly white around the pool.

"Whenever Jay and I turn a spade of dirt or tuck in a new plant, we have the plan to guide us."

As I look back on this long-term project, I believe a professionally designed master plan gave us our money's worth many times over. It allowed us to set priorities, working toward a specific goal. When the time came to deal with pool contractors, we had the plan to convey exactly what we wanted. Whenever Jay and I turn a spade of dirt or tuck in a new plant, we have the plan to guide us.

Most important, the plan gave us an integrated design that I would never have come up with on my own, even with my passion for gardening. I simply would not have thought of the garden rooms, nor could I have made them such graceful extensions of our home's architecture. Although we hired a landscape architect to design a master plan, we have a garden that feels like our own creation because we've been involved every step of the way.

The cutting garden (foreground) provides an attractive transition between the garage and the pool, tying the service area to the surrounding landscape.

KEN DRUSE is one of America's foremost garden writers and photographers. He has authored numerous books, including *The Collector's Garden* and *The Natural Shade Garden.*

Keeping Up with a Changing Garden

(LEFT) To keep paths from being obscured, plants may have to be pruned or moved. The path tapers as it leads from the house, making the garden feel larger.

(INSET) When the garden was first planted, neighboring properties were still visible. Now, mature trees and other plants screen this view.

BEFORE BREAKING ground on my 21-by-50-ft. Brooklyn garden, I knew it would change as it matured. After all, trees grow tall, shrubs fill out, vines climb high. I just didn't realize how dramatic some of the changes would be. Plants well-suited to my site have been all too happy to outgrow it, and my passion for new plants has had to be curbed as much as any sprawling shrub.

I've had to learn ways to cope with, and sometimes even plan for, change in my garden. In fact, I've even learned to expect the unexpected—like the Lady Banks' rose, which shouldn't have been hardy enough to grow here, but that now covers three stories with masses of butter-cream flowers each May. And there's the bamboo that escaped despite my efforts to control it in sunken containers. At times like these I'm reminded that I'm the junior partner in this enterprise with nature.

A Landscape Plan Helps You Evaluate Changes

The only sunny area is the place for growing sun-loving plants. They include a tall oakleaf hydrangea, (*Hydrangea quercifolia*), *Astilbe* 'Superba', and Asiatic lilies.

As trees grew, shade was created. Here, gardeners' garters (*Phalaris arundinacea* var. *picta*) and variegated knotweed (*Persicaria virginiana* 'Variegatum') bring light to this shady area.

A waterfall spills into a kidney-shaped pond, which is now being expanded. Reshaping this area will transform the entire garden.

A gateway to the garden performs double duty as an arbor. The Japanese wisteria is pruned often to keep it from taking over.

Nursery purchases waiting to be planted in the garden find a temporary home in containers near the back door. A black jardiniere holds a tiny water garden.

Mudroom

House

The author wanted cozy seating in the garden. A rustic bench by David Robinson nestles under forsythia growing over a metal arch.

In 1987, I thought I would design this garden, plant it, then just enjoy it. But I've come to realize that I don't really want the garden to ever be finished—certainly not my involvement with it. Its ever-changing nature excites me and draws me into an ongoing process of discovery and responsiveness.

SIZE UP YOUR TURF

The thrill of planting is often irresistible, but it pays to get acquainted with the site of your future garden before digging too many holes. I was lucky that I moved to my new home in the fall. I had time to do only a little cleanup before being forced by weather to spend several months observing and contemplating the plot.

Getting to know the site helped me to learn about its growing conditions. I discovered the direction of winter winds. I analyzed the existing soil. I measured the space and noted any fixed features that could be seen in winter. I recorded patterns of light and shade. While this is critical in the early stages of garden-making, it's just as valuable to keep noting changes in available light as the garden evolves.

PONDER HOW YOU'LL USE THE SPACE

While your garden will certainly change over the years, it helps to list up-front what you, and others who will use the space, might want from it. I included both nuts-and-bolts requirements and my most imaginative dreams.

For my garden, I wanted places to sit, entertain, and cook outdoors. I hoped to screen unwanted views and city sounds without blocking light or air circulation. Most of all, I planned to use as much space as possible to indulge my appetite for plants.

At this stage, I could envision 1001 possibilities—about 990 too many for this tiny rectangle. So I made some key design decisions. The patio would be next to the house. Vertical garden space for growing vines could be created with trellises, arbors, and lines stretched between hooks.

The largest planted area would be in the center of the yard, bisected by a narrow paved walk. I fantasized about having a little pond with a waterfall. I envisioned a raised area at the rear of the garden where the path would end at the steps of a classical stone temple.

SKETCH ROUGH PLANS

On second thought, I decided that an elegant folly wouldn't jibe with its surroundings. But as I drew garden plans, a temple of sorts emerged as a circle of trees on higher ground.

Using photocopies of the "base plan" of my site, I sketched many ideas. When I looked at my drawings, I wished they were more inspiring. But don't worry if your plan isn't pretty or artistic. The point is to see how the things you imagine might fit together with the space and with each other. My drawings served the important purpose of designing the garden's skeleton or structure. If a garden has "good bones," even some shaggy plantings won't diminish it.

> *"Another way to keep a garden cohesive as it evolves is to adopt a design theme or guiding principle."*

As the garden changes, the structure still shows through, even when covered by snow.

Since a small space is less flexible than a larger landscape, I wanted to come as close as I could to a final plan before planting anything. This is difficult and, frankly, against my inclination to let my imagination—and plants—run free. I tried to visualize myself in the space. I closed my eyes and thought about how I would enter and leave the garden. How much room was around me when I strolled the path? What might I see as I walked through the space and looked to the left, right, down, and up?

CONSIDER A THEME

Another way to keep a garden cohesive as it evolves is to adopt a design theme or guiding principle. This can be based on a garden style, a color palette, specific growing conditions, or some other unifying motif for a specific area or an entire garden. A theme helps me to rein in my urge to haphazardly acquire every enticing plant.

I hoped to create the character of a woodland within the rigid geometry of an urban rectangle. And I wanted to play with the illusion that the garden was roomy. The boundaries were set, but I could accentuate the garden's length. For example, paving stones for the path were arranged so their width tapered as they led from the house, making the distance seem longer.

Bluestone slabs discovered on the site transformed an area for dining. Over time, plantings have softened the edges.

looked unbelievably lush. The plants loved the newly amended soil, and the shelter the surrounding buildings afforded.

I tend to let plants do what they naturally do, but I learned that in the tight quarters of this garden, my wards—especially shrubs and vines—would need much attention. Whatever the style and scale of a garden, some pruning and training of plants is usually needed just to keep plants healthy. I also had to keep the cozy jungle from strangling itself. I could see that letting one plant go wild might mean the loss of another from overcrowding.

Methodical pruning tamed certain plants, such as the Japanese wisteria (*Wisteria floribunda*), which is confined to a small space. About once a month, I trim the vine back to spurs four or five nodes in length away from main shoots. It blooms without fail every spring.

FEEL FREE TO MOVE— OR REMOVE—PLANTS

As this garden has grown, I've had to face that there were simply too many big plants for the space. Trees and shrubs eventually shaded out some of the understory.

Coping with excess growth in a crowded garden may challenge a gardener beyond the quandary of which branch to trim. Even a simple process like dividing healthy perennials involves making decisions. If I don't have space to plant offshoots, I pass them on to friends, or donate them to a plant sale. A few plants get carted off to the compost bin. However, what can be especially daunting is removing a large, well-loved plant. Arboricide is among the most difficult acts a plant lover can execute. But it isn't always necessary.

Over the years, I've realized that nearly any plant can be moved. With advance planning, you can do an especially good job. It's best to

Like a room with a high ceiling, the garden appears larger if plantings around the outside edges direct the view toward the interior and up to the sky. This also enhances the air of privacy, a key consideration, and makes it seem like a clearing in the woods.

KEEP PLANTS FROM TAKING OVER

While a garden's plan may not change for centuries, plants do. Shrubs from my former roof garden that had stayed small in pots suddenly took off. The cutleaf sumac (*Rhus typhina* 'Laciniata'), which was under 3 ft. tall after six years, doubled in size its first year in the ground. By the second summer, the garden

> *"No matter how much I love to garden, there are times when paralysis sets in."*

trim the roots of shrubs and trees a year before you intend to move them by plunging a spade straight into the ground in a circle around the plant. When you lift the plant in early spring, try to keep the root ball intact. Replant it as soon as possible, and water well for the entire first season.

Unfortunately, I can't always plan that far ahead. But I'm still willing to move any plant nearly any time in the growing season by taking certain precautions. I dig up as much of the root mass as possible and prune the top growth to compensate for roots left behind.

Plants moved in autumn need a thick mulch the first winter. Perennials benefit from a little shade from a row cover or a piece of cardboard for a week or so. And all transplants need lots of water.

If you don't have room within your garden, there's the problem of finding a new home for a cherished plant. Fortunately, there seems to be a gardener born every minute, and someone will want your plant—especially if it's unusual.

TOO MANY TASKS?
JUST DO SOMETHING

No matter how much I love to garden, there are times when paralysis sets in. I've wandered aimlessly around the garden or—worse yet— avoided setting foot into it because I'm overwhelmed by too much to do. My cure for this is to start a simple task—even repotting one plant. Once I'm in motion, I slide to the next thing without even noticing and, before I know it, three hours have gone by and I've accomplished a lot. Making a list can also get me started, and I often do many things that aren't even on the list.

Sometimes when I've been working too hard, and become garden-blind—unable to see what's been done or needs doing—I'll invite friends over for a tour. The invitation spurs me to spruce things up quickly. But, more than that, as I walk around, pointing things out, listening to responses and answering questions, I see my garden with fresh eyes. I notice successes, like exquisite, serendipitous combinations, more than problems.

EXPECT SURPRISES

Unexpected events will alter a garden. When trees fall or vines tumble, we gardeners have to rise to the occasion. New options appear. Decisions must be made.

In my case, one of the five trees in the circle at the rear of the garden turned out to have been mislabeled. The allegedly sterile tree set fruit, but the real calamity is that it grew twice as fast as its comrades, stealing their moisture and plunging them into shade. I decided to sacrifice the other four to make room for the one big one.

The greatest upheaval happened just last year. The pond sprang a leak. The PVC liner, guaranteed for six years, ultimately crumbled in its tenth. Since I've found that pools are often too small but rarely too large, the new pond will be twice as big as the old one. And the whole garden will be transformed once it's finished.

CREATIVE
APPROACHES

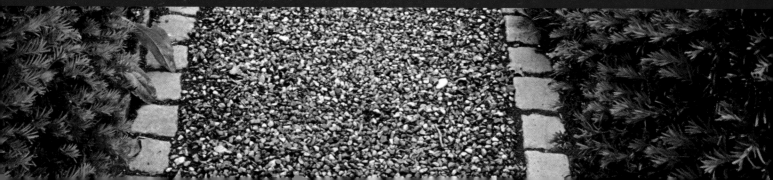

2

NOW THAT YOU'VE LEARNED about the step-by-step process of landscape design, we'll take a look at some of the creative approaches used by designers to work with outdoor spaces.

Is your home symmetrical or asymmetrical? Your answer will help you apply the twin principles of landscape layout to your property. You'll learn to divide and conquer—turning your yard into a series of smaller garden rooms that can be tackled one at a time and designed to suit your family's varied needs, interests, and desires. You'll learn how to connect these spaces by creating a series of garden passageways that draw you from one garden room to another and how to add interest to these garden rooms by creating eye-catching focal points.

Finally, we'll explore the inspirational side of design and learn how to adapt the many lessons provided by nature—whether it's how to combine plants effectively or make the most of natural light.

The Twin Principles of Landscape Layout

RICHARD IVERSEN

is a Professor of Ornamental Horticulture at The State University of New York, where he teaches courses and manages a two-acre display garden. He is the author of *The Exotic Garden.*

An asymmetric house is best complemented by the relaxed lines of a natural-looking garden. Plantings that echo the random patterns of nature create a harmonious setting for this rambling home.

THE BEST-DESIGNED GARDENS are those with colors, textures and shapes that, when combined, echo the features of the house they surround. But because a house cannot be visually separated from its garden, finding a way to make the two look good together can be one of the most perplexing dilemmas a gardener faces.

As a professor of horticulture and a garden designer, I have pondered this problem and have devised some simple guidelines to help with the design of gardens suitable for any style of house.

I teach my students that every garden is made up of two main components: open space and details (plants). How the space and plants are combined determines a garden's style. Similarly, every house has open space within its walls; and *details*, such as doors, windows and trim. The way an architect or builder arranges that space and those details determines the style of a house.

SYMMETRIC GARDEN

Architectural accents in a symmetric garden are more formal and reflect the house style.

Focals points are effectively placed at the end of a straight path to draw you through the garden.

Symmetric gardens are balanced, with neatly manicured, matching plants on either side of a path.

In symmetric gardens, straight central walkways are essential.

Symmetric Georgian-Style House

For the sake of simplicity, I've divided house and garden styles into two basic types: *symmetric* style (also called "formal") and *asymmetric* style (also called "informal"). One or the other will apply to any house and garden.

SYMMETRIC STYLES ARE GEOMETRICALLY BALANCED

Study the front of your house from your yard—if the windows and decorative trim on each side mirror one another and are equally spaced on either side of a centered front door, your house has a symmetric design. Although this arrangement of doors and windows brands a house of any vintage as symmetric, historic architectural styles such as Palladian, Georgian, Federal, Greek-revival and Colonial-revival are prime examples. These architectural styles are frequently ornamented with decorative treatments above doors and windows, and porches supported by columns like those in ancient Greek and Roman temples. The classical influence is also apparent in symmetric gardens.

For the sake of compatibility, a symmetric house needs a symmetric or formal garden. These are distinguished by plants arranged in a mirror image on each side of a primary axis, such as a walkway leading from the street to the front door. Space on each side of the walk may feature a single flower border or several geometric beds arranged in rectangles, squares, trapezoids or triangles

Plants in a symmetric garden should be in an orderly geometric arrangement—neatness is the rule. Plants should be manicured, even to the point of being clipped into geometric or topiary shapes. The most suitable site for a symmetrical garden is on level or terraced ground.

The boundaries of a symmetric garden are straight lines parallel and perpendicular to the central walk, and may be further defined by wrought-iron or picket fences, or by clipped hedges.

A principal feature of a formal garden is an art object that serves as a focal point, or "terminus." Its placement is important to the suc-

Geometric boundaries outline symmetric gardens, such as these square walls of clipped hedges.

ASYMMETRIC GARDEN

In an asymmetric garden, paths are often left unedged to better mimic a natural setting.

Plantings are balanced by the repetition of color on either side of the path.

In an asymmetric design, plants are left to grow in their natural form rather than sheared into shape.

Winding paths and spreading plants are key to asymmetric design.

cess of the design, so it is usually positioned at the end of a path or at the intersection of two paths. Widening a path around such a feature will increase its importance. Statues, sundials, birdbaths, fountains, furniture or gazebos can all be focal points. Classical motifs, such as statues of Greek or Roman deities, enhance houses with similar features. Ornate Italian-style urns—such as Borghese and Medici—planted with stiff, architectural plants—such as agaves or yuccas—are also traditional choices, as are simply shaped Italian terra-cotta pots.

"The hallmark of the asymmetric garden is a subtle yet artistic harmony in which the hand of man is unrecognizable."

ASYMMETRIC STYLES MIMIC RANDOMNESS OF NATURE

The asymmetric garden is commonly called an "informal," "natural," "free-form," "rustic," "wild" or "Oriental" garden. In an asymmetric garden, plants are arranged to simulate the randomness of nature. Asymmetric gardens are appropriate for houses with off-center doors, windows, chimineys or porches.

Andrew Jackson Downing, a 19th-century American landscape designer, advocated asymmetric, romantic-looking landscapes to accompany asymmetrical country cottages and Swiss-style chalets. He enhanced the steeply pitched roofs and odd angles with tall, craggy conifers, jagged rocks and rushing streams. Modernistic, asymmetric houses that take

their inspiration from Asia (such as those designed by Frank Lloyd Wright), and some ranch houses, are suitable for more manicured, but equally rambling and naturalistic Oriental gardens. Rustic-looking ornaments such as twig benches, bridges and gazebos are scattered along meandering paths, rather than placed at the end of a vista as they are in symmetric gardens.

The hallmark of the asymmetric garden is a subtle yet artistic harmony in which the hand of man is unrecognizable. This effect is achieved by skillfully combining natural elements and plants. For example, a rock garden mimics the look of a mountain setting. Woodland and streamside gardens are developed by placing native and other ornamental plants between existing trees.

In an asymmetric garden, plants are again placed on both sides of an axis (path), but the axis is less obvious than it would be in a formal garden. Instead, paths are curved and the plants are grouped in unequal numbers that only appear to be balanced. Garden plants sometimes run wild, partially obscuring a path. They are too vigorous for anything but a wild garden, and their forms echo the informal lines of paths, streams and the house itself.

(ABOVE) A garden that combines elements of two styles often has format structure with informal plantings. Cottage gardens are a perfect example.

(LEFT) Garden ornaments in an asymmetric garden are often rustic in construction.

IT'S POSSIBLE TO MIX AND MATCH SYMMETRIC AND ASYMMETRIC STYLES

Just as some houses mix symmetric and asymmetric elements, so can a garden. The garden in front of the formal portion of the house may echo its style with a geometric enclosed entry courtyard. Outside the enclosure, curving walks may radiate past rock gardens into surrounding woodland gardens.

Match House and Garden with Formal or Informal Design

To design a garden that will complement your house, think of garden plants as part of a big picture–design the whole site as an artist would design a composition for a painting. Include a pleasing background of lawn and flowering plants, provide a sense of enclosure by bordering the garden with a hedge or carefully placed trees, and use paths and views to link the garden to other parts of the grounds and to the house.

DESIGNING A SIMPLE SYMMETRIC GARDEN

The best way to begin a symmetric garden plan is to position the primary and secondary axes, or paths, within a square or rectangular site. The paths link the garden to the house. Start the main axis at a door or window in the house and continue straight to the farthest end of the garden, ending at an important decorative feature such as a planter, sundial, arbor or gate.

Secondary axes that intersect the primary axis add an element of excitement to the design. For a simple formal garden, flank the axes with balanced patches of lawn or flower borders. The size and shape of the borders can be determined by using a proportion of approximately five units width to eight units length. This ratio could yield 5- × 8-ft. beds, or a 10- × 16-ft. bed, for instance.

An array of geometric island beds placed symmetrically around the primary axis and planted with brightly colored flowers forms an appropriate garden for a symmetric or formal house.

Symmetric house

Primary axis

Secondary axis

Planter

Arbor

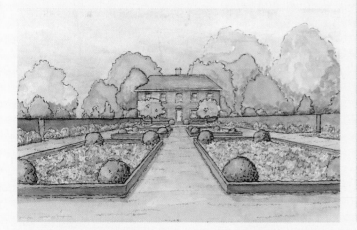

DESIGNING A SIMPLE ASYMMETRIC GARDEN

The existing site will dictate the look of an asymmetric garden. Large trees may call for the sinuous curves of a woodland walk bordered by naturalized spring-flowering bulbs and native wildflowers. Stony outcrops demand a rock garden planted with dwarf conifers and small flowering plants. If drainage is poor, consider a pond or bog garden edged with ferns, native irises and other moisture-loving plants. The path to the door might wind through gardens planted with rhododendrons. Combine changing elevations and winding paths with groups of randomly placed plants to complement the off-center entrance to an asymmetric house.

ASYMMETRIC HOUSE AND GARDEN

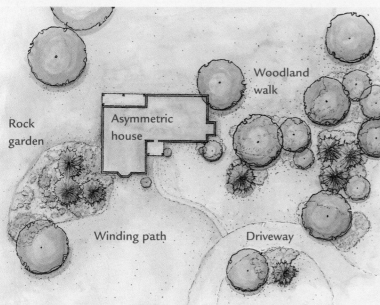

Rock garden

Asymmetric house

Woodland walk

Winding path

Driveway

If a house has mixed styles, match a garden with similar architectural details. Even though this house has asymmetric features, a small symmetric garden works because it is aligned with a straight walk leading to a set of symmetric bay windows.

Plants can take on an informal arrangement within the geometric grid of a formal garden. Such gardens were typical of colonial gardens in America, and were the genius of 19th- and early-20th-century English cottage-garden designers Gertrude Jekyll and Vita Sackville-West.

I have distilled these principles from dozens of sources during a decade of teaching. They can be used to design a new garden or to make an existing one harmonize with the architecture of a house. But when all is said and done, a simple garden is likely to be the best garden.

TARA DILLARD

is a garden designer and lecturer in Atlanta. She contributed to *Gardening 'Round Atlanta,* and has appeared on local television and radio programs to talk about gardening.

Focal Points
Lead the Eye

A single pot can light up the whole garden. Make sure you match it to the scale and style of the rest of the garden.

M Y BACKYARD HAD IT ALL: a bench, a birdbath, a birdfeeder, a birdhouse on a post, wind chimes, a sundial on a pedestal, a wooden swing, baskets hanging from iron poles, a formal herb garden, an arbor over a gate, a botanical garden's diversity of plants, and other objects the years have kindly let me forget.

Obviously, I had not grasped the basic concept of focal points that had been taught in garden design classes: that there should be one main focal point per garden area. What I needed to do was simplify, simplify, simplify. So I wheeled my cobalt-blue wheelbarrow to the backyard, loaded it up with "focal points," and retired them to a spot in the garage. Then I did it again and again. And so a beautiful garden began.

A view through to another view can highlight a focal point. The statue at the end of this allée is eye-catching and so draws you forward and through the garden.

WHAT IS A FOCAL POINT?

As an element of garden design, a focal point is something that draws the eye and provides it with a visual resting place. The focal point is so important that I include it early on in the garden-design process, right up there with trees, paths, and evergreen shrubs. Designing a garden for winter interest first is the best way to make sure it works in every season. In my opinion, a garden must be beautiful all year. In fact, I am demanding enough to expect a garden to be beautiful every hour of every day. Focal points help me achieve this, because, if I plan right, not only is my garden a stand-out in the summer, but when winter arrives I'll still have a lovely garden view of a sundial on a pedestal with a backdrop of evergreen shrubs and a canopy of trees.

There are many different types of focal points. A mature tree form, like contorted filbert (*Corylus avellana*) with its twisted branches and catkins, can be a stunning winter focal point. When using a deciduous plant like contorted filbert, it's best to give it a backdrop of evergreen shrubs, a wall of your house, or a fence so that each delicate feature is highlighted. Most plants used as focal points will require some special attention to pruning to work year-round. They should either be evergreen or have an attractive habit when they are leafless.

Some plants become focal points accidentally. Take hostas. For just three or four days in the fall, they turn an incredible florescent shade of golden-yellow. Those few days of hosta glory are my favorite of their entire year. In the same way, a large grouping of plants can work as a seasonal focal point. Penny McHenry, founder of the American Hydrangea Society, has more than 500 hydrangea plants in her 1-acre garden in Atlanta. In season, these hydrangeas become a resplendent focal point.

But because my time is limited, I prefer that my focal points be very low maintenance or "fixed." Choices for fixed focal points are limitless: statues, pots, sundials, birdbaths, birdhouses, old farm tools, and benches all work well.

Some focal points also offer the added interest of movement. A pond with a fountain provides not only movement, but also sound. A pond without a fountain becomes a reflection pool with images that change by the minute. Another focal point with movement is the mobile, which should be hung from a tree limb. I have even seen animals used as focal points. In Scotland, I witnessed several gardens with long, narrow vistas framed by plants on either side, with sheep grazing at the end. At my local zoo in Atlanta, the plantings are beautifully lush, yet they fade into the background as soon as a peacock fans its tail.

FOCAL POINTS SERVE SEVERAL FUNCTIONS

My favorite focal point is a bench. It attracts the eye and draws the body, serving as both a focal point and a destination. The perfect bench provides a view to another focal point while you're sitting on it. I prefer a wooden bench because it can be welcoming even in winter.

Because they create interest and set a mood, statues can make great focal points, but only if they are in keeping with the scale and style of the site. If you find the right statue but the scale is too small, try raising it on a pedestal. A large statue can work in a small area if you design the garden carefully and are a fan of drama. I like the look of aged statues best, a look I can achieve by using buttermilk mixed with tomato fertilizer as a top-coating on stone, terra cotta, and concrete.

A view through to another view is a popular way to create a garden room. The first "view through" is typically an arch, arbor, stone terrace, lawn, pair of pots, or pair of evergreen shrubs. The second view might be the main focal point, and tends to be a bench or a statue that beckons the eye and body.

Empty pots make excellent focal points. They are also low maintenance. But not just any empty pot works as a focal point. It must have intrinsic character and good form. Most empty pots used as focal points need to be placed on a pedestal. Bricks make good pedestals because you can easily control their height.

A classic pot is the terra-cotta oil jar. It can be placed upright or on its side, completely changing the scale and mood of the garden area. I used a pair of pots with removable lids to create an entryway to a new part of my garden. When I plant the pots for the different seasons I go dramatic: something tall with lots of color and lush trailing plants.

The versatility of planted pots creates a great dynamic for a focal point. If you demand a beautiful, low-maintenance garden with color and drama, then your design equation should be trees, evergreen shrubs, and a large

A fountain increases the interest of a fixed focal plant. Symmetrical plantings frame the view of this fountainhead.

Focal points can be combined to intensify visual interest. The reflected image of this dramatic gazebo increases its impact.

focal-point pot planted with color. A single pot that's planted with an obscene amount of colorful flowers will give the illusion that the entire garden space is colorful. A practice common in English gardens is to enlarge an area where two paths intersect, place a large pot on a pedestal in the middle, and plant it with lots of color. This not only adds a jolt of color, but it also brings a new dimension of scale to the garden area because the eye is drawn up from the surrounding plantings.

USE FOCAL POINTS TO PLAY WITH SPATIAL PERCEPTIONS

Perception is not reality in a garden. To make a small garden area seem larger you should use fine-textured or small-leaved plant material and colors like blue and burgundy that recede into the background. The same is true of choosing a focal point. When copying a 1920's garden for a client, I couldn't exactly replicate the use of a white marble bench because the space I was working with was much smaller. A bench would have been too wide, and white marble would have jumped forward, not receded. The solution was a dark-colored bird-

bath that was the right height and became a part of the garden because of the azalea foliage that enveloped its base.

A short pathway leading to a statue can appear longer if you make your path wider at the start and slightly narrower at its end, creating an exaggerated perspective. The statue should be small and of a receding color like lead, verdi gris, or black.

Another way to manipulate a small garden space is with the back or side property lines. A tapestry hedge (a mix of several types of shrubs and trees) planted in an old-fashioned manner (not straight across) along the property line with an interesting gate will provide a focal point and the illusion of more garden through the gate. The plantings should actually touch each gatepost, and a flagstone path should lead to the gate. A pair of cone-shaped evergreens (cone-shaped plants draw the eye more than those that are rounded) placed on either side of the gate will further emphasize the gate.

A garden mirror is a great device for creating the appearance of depth in a garden space where little exists. In a tiny woodland garden that has a fence, I hung a huge window with mirrors instead of glass. A vine grows thickly on the fence and encircles the window. The mirrors let you see another woodland, which in reality is only a reflection. If your house has a large, blank wall, consider hanging a mirrored faux French door on it, as the beckoning nature of entryways makes them successful focal points. If you have a favorite color, installing a faux French door is your opportunity to use it. From a distance, a mirrored faux French door that's painted cobalt blue with a path leading to it and a pair of boxwoods on either side looks very real.

PAY CAREFUL ATTENTION TO PLACEMENT

It's usually a good idea to stick with just one major focal point in each garden area or room. Trying to incorporate many focal points into your garden can be a challenge. One of the tricks I use is to let the tips of some plants just touch the focal point, tying it more intrinsically to its site. A stone rabbit, for example, placed next to a planted pot looks best if it is just touching some of the trailing foliage with its face as if it were having a nibble.

Several objects placed together can create a focal point. This is called a garden vignette. Garden vignettes are fun because they allow you to be original and create a mood. An effective vignette I recently saw included an antique chimney pipe, antique watering can, and a sturdy woven basket placed at the entry to a garden work area. It gave the illusion that nearby flowers were watered from the can and that the gardener could just grab the basket and be off to cut a few flowering stems.

As I mentioned before, a focal point should be in harmony with the scale and style of its site. I didn't always know this. After seeing one in a friend's garden, I desperately wanted a stacked-quartz, stone pedestal with a sundial

A mirror placed in just the right spot creates the illusion of a larger garden.

resting on top. I knew exactly where to put it, on axis with the center of the bay window in my living room. When the big day arrived, the hired help handled the stone exactly as I instructed them. Yet the result was a disaster. My house is red brick, and the flat-topped stone pedestal was in the middle of my formal herb garden. I had not captured the proper style or scale of my garden. So out went the stones and in went a terra-cotta, fluted column pedestal with a planted pot topping it, not a flat sundial. Now scale and style are in harmony.

When you are farther away from the house the rule of scale and style can usually be ignored. A woodland garden can become graceful and elegant with the addition of a formal stone pedestal topped by a large, empty French container. In this case, the formality in an informal setting is both a surprise and an invitation to venture forth.

Before I purchase an object to serve as a focal point, I apply "The Tara Test." As my hand reaches for the item, I always stop and ask myself: "Is this focal point heirloom quality? Will people fight over it at my estate sale?" Only if my answer is yes to both questions do I buy it.

To create a garden room, start by creating a sense of enclosure with hedges, walls, or fences. Then spruce up the space with color, texture, and a touch of personality. Here, a gate serves as a doorway into a soothing space (photo taken at A on site plan), while in another area, a chair offers a place to sit for a spell.

SHARON DENSMORE

is an interior designer in Charleston, South Carolina. She approaches the spaces around her home much as she does indoor spaces—by creating and decorating a series of rooms.

Design Garden
Rooms
That Beckon

WHEN MY GRANDPARENTS gave me a set of oil paints for my tenth birthday, my first paintings were of imaginary gardens. I had already been picturing magical garden rooms as I spent many hours on a swing that overlooked the gardens on their farm in northern Maine. A few years ago my daughter Kristen found those old paintings in a cabinet. When she showed them to her dad, he said, "Your mother was designing our garden 40 years ago!" That wasn't quite true, but there are certainly elements of those childhood pictures in the garden I have today.

Even as a child, I never liked seeing plants just randomly placed. I always wanted some kind of structure to anchor and define a garden space. I've found that making a garden into a room can create a sense of intimacy and encourage relaxed lingering. Garden rooms can draw visitors forward to discover where the sound of water is coming from, where

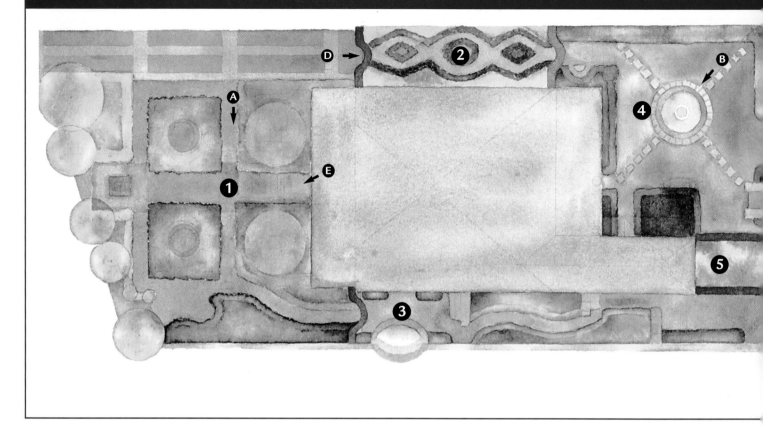

Live in your garden rooms. The author collects flowers from her English garden to arrange for a dinner party in her courtyard.

paths might lead, or what's on the other side of a tall hedge or gate. It's also possible to designate a space for a specific purpose, or as a transitional space akin to a hallway or foyer. Defining garden areas as rooms can also make it easier to focus on designing and financing one space at a time.

CREATE PRIVACY AND INTRIGUE BY ENCLOSING A SPACE

After years of decorating homes as well as making gardens, I've come to believe that both interior and exterior spaces can be approached in similar ways. Whether indoors or outside, the elements of a space should all interrelate harmoniously. I try to achieve this by paying attention to both the architectural structure and the details or "accessories" of a room.

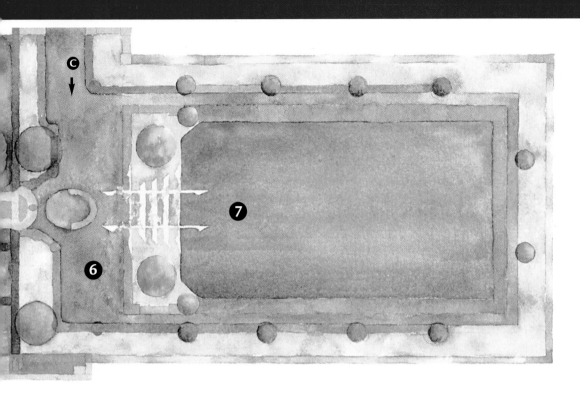

Seven interconnected garden rooms were designed and planted in stages over a period of eight years around this Charleston home. Each room exudes a distinct personality, although many design elements are repeated from room to room. The rooms are connected by a series of paths and include

1 Formal front garden
2 Herb garden
3 Italian-inspired room
4 Semitropical courtyard
5 Staging area/future conservatory
6 Back foyer
7 English-style garden

Just as houses have walls, floors, and ceilings, garden rooms must have defined parameters. These structural "bones" are important in every season. They can anchor and accent lush growth in the summer or reveal sculptural detail in winter.

Structure in a garden can be created with plantings, such as yew or boxwood hedges, evergreen topiaries, trees planted in a specific pattern, or even turfgrass or ground covers. Space can also be delineated with hardscape, such as walkways, walls, fences, pergolas, trellises, arbors, or even seating. Generally, the structure of a garden room combines both plants and hardscaping materials.

One way to begin enclosing a garden is to use the walls of the house or other structures as a starting point. When we bought our

Set the mood with focal points and accessories. Although a classical fountain forms the centerpiece of this courtyard, lush plants and bold-colored chairs give the room a relaxed atmosphere (B on site plan).

Designate a room for a specific function. This transitional area is designed as a foyer with garden benches placed to catch shade (C on site plan).

Use doorways to separate rooms and pique the interest of visitors. A door or gate can create intrigue about what lies beyond it.

home in downtown Charleston 10 years ago, I basically started with a blank slate. The yard was wide open and the few plantings there were destroyed by Hurricane Hugo soon after we moved in. I envisioned a garden that was not readily visible from the street, that would feel like a secret garden away from the noise and stress of city life. I also wanted a garden where everything isn't revealed at once. So I created a framework in which seven gardens surround the house, flowing from one into another (site plan, pp. 70–71). To accomplish this, I started out by enclosing the entire space.

First, I had to decide what materials would be appropriate for the outside "walls" of this space. Since the first level of the house is brick

A Room Is a Room, Whether It's in a House or Garden

To design a garden room, draw from plants, hardscaping, furnishings, and garden accessories to structure and decorate your space. The following are some examples of useful materials.

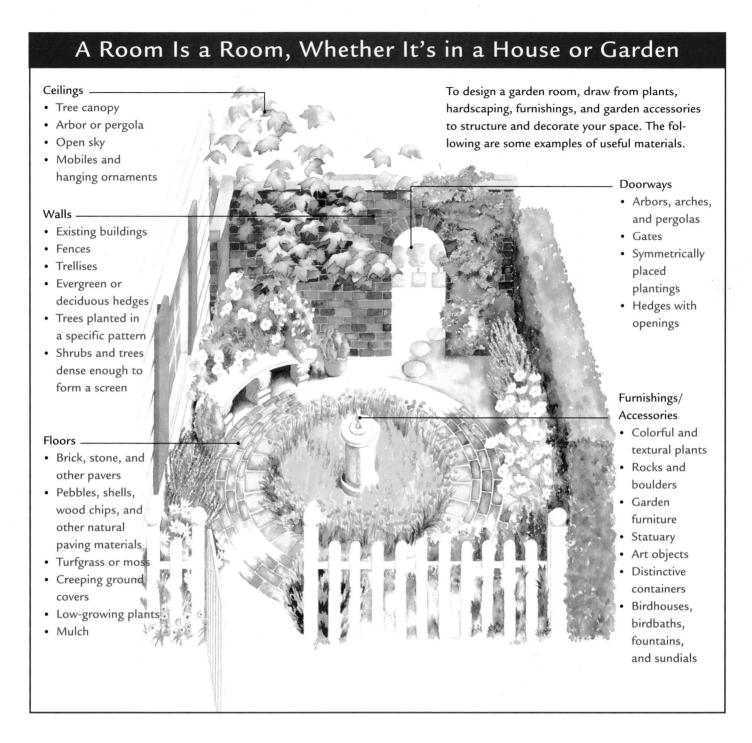

Ceilings
- Tree canopy
- Arbor or pergola
- Open sky
- Mobiles and hanging ornaments

Walls
- Existing buildings
- Fences
- Trellises
- Evergreen or deciduous hedges
- Trees planted in a specific pattern
- Shrubs and trees dense enough to form a screen

Floors
- Brick, stone, and other pavers
- Pebbles, shells, wood chips, and other natural paving materials
- Turfgrass or moss
- Creeping ground covers
- Low-growing plants
- Mulch

Doorways
- Arbors, arches, and pergolas
- Gates
- Symmetrically placed plantings
- Hedges with openings

Furnishings/ Accessories
- Colorful and textural plants
- Rocks and boulders
- Garden furniture
- Statuary
- Art objects
- Distinctive containers
- Birdhouses, birdbaths, fountains, and sundials

and stucco, and the top stories are wood frame with white columns supporting double porches, I decided on a 3-ft.-high, brick coping wall with a 7-ft.-high picket fence supported at intervals by brick-and-stucco piers. These materials relate to the house and the height is proportionate to it as well. This structure runs across the front and around one side of the garden. The wall on the other side, made of

brick and stucco, is 10 ft. high. Its mass helps to anchor all the outside walls to the ground. Within the garden, I also created a wall with a yew hedge to separate the driveway—which is used as a utility area—from the front garden.

If your property slopes or has different levels, what might seem like a challenge can actually make it easier to design distinct spaces. Garden rooms can be created by emphasizing

BEFORE

DURING

HERBS

AFTER

A narrow side yard becomes an herb garden. This garden room is defined by walls including a side of the house, wooden fencing, and a brick wall. The floor is made of brick pathways surrounding geometric beds. An arched doorway now leads into the lush herb garden (D on site plan).

shifts in grade with dividing walls made from either hardscape or plant materials. Steps—with or without doorways—can lead from one room to another. The changes in grade on our property inspired me to create a sunken courtyard leading to a raised area with an English-style garden.

Achieving a balanced sense of scale is essential to creating a harmonious garden room. As with the fences and walls, permanent plants need to be in proper proportion to the objects they're meant to complement. It's especially important when working with an enclosed space to consider what a plant's size will be at maturity. I also focus on sight lines, both from seated and standing positions, to make a room appealing on a human scale.

DECIDE ON EACH ROOM'S STYLE

Another key design consideration is the style of a garden room. Should it be formal or informal, whimsical or eclectic? Should it reflect a specific theme or combine several elements? In choosing a style for a garden room, think about how the space will be used. Also consider the feelings you'd like the room to inspire. Sometimes a color scheme emerges as part of this theme, or a base of colors that can be enhanced with changing annuals or seasonal blooms.

I like many different styles of gardens, so by having separate rooms I am able to play with diverse design elements. I often begin with traditional design conventions, but I also play with incongruous elements and often break the rules. I believe that a private garden should be a place for personal expression. Experimenting is a big part of the fun.

Our house has a formal feel to it, but it doesn't have elaborate details. So I designed

"I like many different styles of gardens, so by having separate rooms I am able to play with diverse design elements."

the front garden as a formal parterre with boxwood hedges, but softened the look by filling the box-rimmed beds with exuberant and colorful plantings. The other rooms also include formal elements, such as a central fountain with classical statuary, but the plantings tend to be lush and flowing.

GIVE EACH ROOM ITS OWN DISTINCT PERSONALITY

Once the "bones" of a room are in place, I concentrate on details that help set the mood. To instill an inviting atmosphere, I like to give each space its own personality. Rooms intended as living spaces benefit from cozy conversation areas with comfortable seating. Carefully chosen garden ornaments can serve as focal points or help to establish a specific mood. I may create an intimate vignette for contemplation by placing a piece of statuary near seating. Or I may add a touch of whimsy to draw the eye or create a playful mood.

Just as I place floral arrangements to enhance interior rooms, I use container plantings as accent pieces in the garden. Plants in pots can also be used to introduce a certain color or texture, to change the scale in a bed, or to pull a section of a border together. I often enjoy moving containers from room to room, letting my intuition guide me in choosing the most pleasing placement for that season.

The geometry of this parterre garden is defined by low, clipped hedges and tall evergreens. This garden room is meant to be viewed from above on the front porch (E on site plan).

CREATE CONTINUITY BETWEEN YOUR HOUSE AND GARDEN

To create a sense of "flow" between a house and garden, it helps to use hardscaping materials that relate to the age and style of your home. Repeating architectural elements of the house, such as arches or defined angles, also reinforces continuity.

Since we live in a historic house, whenever possible I make use of old materials to create a feeling of aged maturity. These include salvaged brick in the paving and walls; antique ironwork in gates, tables, chairs, and wall ornaments; and antique urns and statuary. The same principle can also be applied to plant choices. For example, I grow old roses and many old varieties of plants.

Although each room should have its own theme or personality, repeating design elements helps to create continuity. Each of my garden rooms includes fragrant vines, colorful annuals, night-blooming flowers, and herbs. I find that recurring fragrances also enhance a sense of harmony as you walk through adjoining spaces. In addition, I repeat color themes and textures from room to room. Although I love to draw from a huge palette of colors, I've used plants with pale-pink to deep-red flowers throughout the garden as a unifying base scheme.

Whenever possible, I employ the same craftspeople in each phase of garden construction. This can establish consistency in style and workmanship, and can even promote creative collaboration. For example, my brick-

"I find that recurring fragrances also enhance a sense of harmony as you walk through adjoining spaces."

mason suggested building the brick wall in the English garden to look like an antique ruin with planting pockets tucked within it.

LIVE IN YOUR GARDEN ROOMS AND LET THEM EVOLVE

I believe that gardens should stir the emotions, delight the senses, trigger pleasant memories, and inspire new associations. Since garden rooms are meant to be lived in, include whatever elements will make you feel at home. Think about what you like most about the rooms of your home and other spaces you find pleasing, and try to bring these elements into your garden. Then sit back and bask in the rooms you create.

Before my husband's death last year, we had always spent countless hours in the garden, dining or just relaxing. One of Dick's greatest pleasures was observing changes in the garden from day to day. He loved watching birds and butterflies play with our two Himalayan house cats and watching for Henrietta, our resident hummingbird who seemed to arrive by magic on the same day every summer. Since his death, I've gained solace and strength from being in my soul-soothing, outdoor rooms. I cherish memories of times we spent here together and let the garden inspire me to make new changes from day to day.

∾

"The element of mystery is one of five intriguing characteristics of natural landscapes."

DARREL MORRISON

is a professor of landscape architecture at the University of Georgia. He designed the gardens at the Lady Bird Johnson Wildflower Center and was the senior landscape planner for the Utah State Botanical Center.

Adapt *Design* Lessons *from Nature*

Nature teaches landscaping: The author's students paint natural scenes in watercolor to use as reference for garden designs.

W HEN I FIRST SAW THIS wooded acreage of the Georgia Piedmont that overlooked the broad, meandering Oconee River, it seemed inevitable that I'd put down roots in this wild place. From where I stood, on a gigantic, lichen-covered boulder on the shoreline, I could see that the river disappeared around a bend, and I was intrigued by thoughts of the unseen, mysterious landscape.

The element of mystery—of not knowing what's around the bend—is one of five intriguing characteristics of natural landscapes that I have distilled from a quarter century of observing nature and teaching landscape architecture at the University of Georgia and the University of Wisconsin.

You, like my students, can record plant distribution patterns, such as drifts and curving patterns of plants along river banks, and intimate details of foliage and bark in pen or watercolors, so that the natural design elements can be reinterpreted in a garden design.

The next step is to look carefully at your own garden site. Note its environmental characteristics in a site-plan drawing. Also examine the type of soil in your garden, the slope of the ground, the amount of available light and moisture, and any microclimates your garden may have.

Then, create a drawing on tracing paper to overlay your existing site drawing. I call this a mass/space plan. The "mass" can be new groups of tall grasses, shrubs or trees laid out in shapes that are similar to the plant-distribution shapes recorded in your watercolor. The "space" in your overlay can include open, noncanopied areas.

After the existing masses and spaces are arranged on your drawing, you can distribute new plants and seeds in your garden in ways that simulate the design elements of plants growing in nature as recorded in your watercolors.

PATTERNS:
Groups of a Single Species

There is a common misconception that natural landscapes are chaotic and lacking in perceptible patterns. But in relatively undisturbed, naturally evolving landscapes, pattern is ever-present—not in the form of orchard-like grids of trees but in the subtle arrangements of plants.

In nature, most plant species are aggregated, or grouped, with others of the same species. Plants are grouped together because they have very specific environmental needs that can be

In nature, plants grow in patterns, or drifts. Drifts are clumps of a single species that are dense in the center and widely spaced toward the edges. (BELOW) Pink evening primroses (*Oenothera speciosa*) blend into wild Texas bluebonnets (*Lupinus texensis*). (BELOW RIGHT) A garden planted in drifts of blue bugle-weed (*Ajuga reptans*).

met only in certain areas, or because their means of reproduction results in the seed falling near the parent.

With either vegetative or seed reproduction, there is a tendency for plants to form these natural "drifts." A drift is simply a group of plants with a higher density in the center and a feathered edge of more widely spaced plants. In the garden this characteristic is easily translated into naturalized drifts of flowering bulbs or drifts of annuals and perennials that are allowed to self-sow.

A SENSE OF PLACE:
Regional Landscapes

Because soil, climate and topography vary from region to region throughout the country, each region has distinctive plant communities. And within a single site there may be several different microhabitats, such as cool, moist, shady areas or areas of exposed, rocky soil. Unique combinations of plants adapt to each type of regional environment.

The tendency for gardeners to use a relatively small number of widely adapted, often exotic species results in gardens with an uninteresting, mass-produced look. Gardens can be enriched by introducing the regional identity and subtle plant diversity of their surrounding natural landscapes.

Regional identity enriches gardens. Incorporating the surrounding natural landscape into a garden adds interest, as shown in this woodland garden (LEFT) and Southwestern garden (BELOW).

"*Plant detail is abundant in nature and should be consciously included in a garden design.*"

MYSTERY:
Partially Concealed Views

The spaces carved into a natural landscape by a meandering river provide a useful analogy for garden design. In a garden setting, curved beds that broaden along the outside of the curve, and have "peninsulas" of vegetation on the inside of the curve, subtly block a view. This partial concealment provides mystery and intrigue mimicking the patterns of rivers. In a garden, these flowing spaces may sometimes be translated literally as waterways, but more often they will be represented by a curving path or bed of low-growing perennials. The taller vegetation of the "peninsulas" along these "rivers" can be tall perennials, grasses, shrubs or even trees, if space permits.

A wild river landscape has mysterious appeal. The unseen landscape around a river's bend provides intrigue and invites exploration. Adapting its curves to a garden yields similar results.

CHANGE OVER TIME:
A Maturing Landscape

Change is an integral part of the natural landscape—not only the seasonal changes that come with new growth, flowering, seed production, changing foliage colors and leaf fall, but also long-term changes associated with the reproduction and spread of plants, the colonization of new arrivals and the death of mature plants. I like to encourage

A partially concealed garden is naturally mysterious. A curving gravel path, mimicking the meandering course of a river, has "peninsulas" of tall vegetation that block views and invite visitors to explore the garden further.

A maturing landscape is a place of discovery: Changes in nature and in the garden, such as colonizing basket of gold (*Aurinia saxatilis*) and purple *Aubrieta deltoidea* and the death of mature trees in this garden, give the landscape an appealing, ever-changing look.

gardeners to nurture this element of change in their gardens by incorporating such elements as fallen trees and self-sown volunteer plants where possible. The more traditional approach of "freezing" a landscape at a particular stage of development costs a gardener considerable energy and resources—not to mention the boredom of it all.

INTRICACY:
Details of Bark and Leaf

Plant detail is abundant in nature and should be consciously included in a garden design. Fine-bladed grasses and fern fronds, textural mosses and lichens, and the slender webbing of deciduous twigs and branches in winter are among the abundant

intricacies that you can see in nature. Such details can enrich any garden setting.

I discovered that studying nature can provide inspiration for designing natural-looking gardens that are distinctive to a region and ecologically sound. The first step in creating such a garden is, logically enough, familiarizing yourself with the landscapes in nearby natural areas. Even without an instructor like me looking over your shoulder, you can try this exercise.

Texture and detail as seen in nature can enrich a garden. Here, a gardener has mixed bloodroot (*Sanguinaria canadensis*) with variegated *Hosta* and colorful Japanese painted fern (*Athyrium niponicum 'Pictum'*).

The Art of Making
Less
Seem Like More

ROBERT GILLMORE
is best known for his
naturalistic, one-acre
woodland garden,
Evergreen, at his home
in Goffstown, New
Hampshire. He is the
author of *Beauty All
Around You.*

Berms act as subtle,
natural privacy
screens: Berms like this
one in the author's
front yard, planted
with rhododendrons
and ferns, help block
out unwanted views.

HAVE YOU EVER DREAMED of
your own estate? A place so big and private that you can see only your own land?
A home surrounded by lavish gardens
that stretch as far as you can see.

Properties like that usually require dozens of acres of
land and the services of several full-time gardeners, which
is why they are typically the privilege of the rich. But the
artful use of some basic landscaping ideas can turn a less-
than-1-acre lot into an estate. And once established, that
1-acre estate can be maintained in less time and for less
money than most people spend just tending their lawns.

As a landscape designer, I've advised many clients on
ways to make their small landscapes look more established,
luxurious and private. I created my own New Hampshire
"estate" by designing with six simple concepts. My entire
property is my garden, and I have as much estatelike beauty and privacy as I could want on just under an acre.

BERMS PROVIDE PRIVACY ATTRACTIVELY AND ECONOMICALLY

Most estates are surrounded by groves of trees for privacy; these groves can be several hundred feet thick. If you used that technique on a 1-acre lot, you wouldn't have room left for anything else. That's why small-lot owners who want privacy have to create it, not necessarily with trees but with earth or, more specifically, with berms. Berms are artificial ridges made of fill, topped with loam and planted. A berm (which, of course, is opaque) is usually a better screen than even a 300- or 400-ft.-thick belt of trees, and it takes up only a fraction of the space.

My house is less than 20 ft. from the street and only about 50 to 100 ft. from the houses on either side of it. Yet I seldom see these houses or even passing cars. The reason is a 12-ft.-high, 40-ft.-long berm between my house and my neighbor's house, and another 2- to 10-ft.-high, 130-ft.-long, L-shaped berm that runs along the front of my property and separates it from another neighbor's lot. To give these berms even more height and screening power, I planted their crests with rhodo-

Add interest to the greenery with flowering shrubs, garden ornaments and variegated ground covers. The author's garden is blessed with huge natural boulders, which act as sculptural elements.

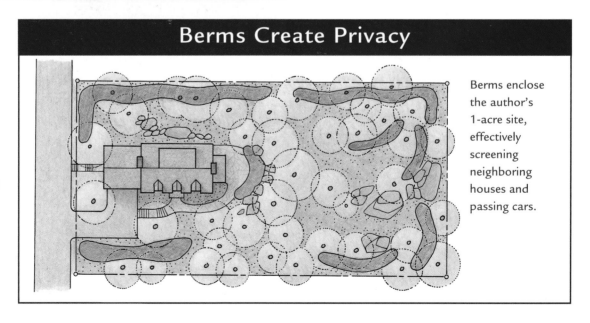

Berms Create Privacy

Berms enclose the author's 1-acre site, effectively screening neighboring houses and passing cars.

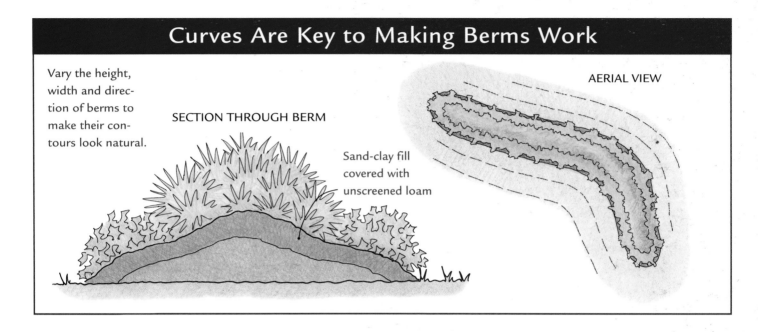

Curves Are Key to Making Berms Work

Vary the height, width and direction of berms to make their contours look natural.

SECTION THROUGH BERM

AERIAL VIEW

Sand-clay fill covered with unscreened loam

dendrons, including rosebay rhododendron (*Rhododendron maximum*), one of the largest species of the genus (up to 12 ft. tall in New England).

Now, instead of seeing asphalt, automobiles and houses, I see growing things —large, lavish drifts of pachysandra, rhododendrons, euonymus and other broad-leaved evergreens. Instead of the trappings of residential development, I am surrounded—truly embraced—by sweeping evergreen walls.

Of course, I could have built fences or walls instead of berms, but a wall higher than 8 ft. is an eyesore. Besides needing regular maintenance, a fence or wall would make my woodland garden look less natural and less like a large estate. Berms, on the other hand, add an interesting, hilly aspect to the garden.

My berms are made of sand-clay fill and covered with unscreened loam. They were graded in a half day by a professional contractor with heavy equipment. Small berms can be shaped in a day using nothing more than hand tools and a wheelbarrow, and you can cut the cost of materials by using debris cleared from your property as fill. You don't even have to wait for the soil to settle before planting. I

planted mine the same day they were installed. For about the same cost as a fence, I made aesthetically pleasing berms that require virtually no maintenance once planted with evergreen shrubs and ground covers.

To make berms look as natural as possible, make sure the slope is not flat but curving, that the crest is not level but undulating, and that the direction is not straight but gently twisting.

NO NEED FOR A HIRED GARDENER WITH LOW-MAINTENANCE PLANTINGS

Many large estates are planted with room-sized beds of carefully tended flowers, hundreds of sculpted shrubs and acres of manicured lawns. It's the most labor-intensive, time-consuming landscape in the world.

But it's possible to have a large garden that is also low maintenance. My lot is extensively

"Most of my garden consists of trees, shrubs and ground covers that, once established, take care of themselves."

This yard needs almost no mowing, pruning or weeding. Trees, shrubs and ground covers make a garden look lush without the need for frequent maintenance.

Keep only as much lawn as you really need. The tiny spot of turf in front of the author's house provides just enough space for sunbathing and reading.

planted with literally thousands of square feet of trees, shrubs and other plants, yet it requires very few hours of maintenance simply because I have almost no lawn and very few annual or perennial flowers. Most of my garden consists of trees, shrubs and ground covers that, once established, take care of themselves. The garden is mulched by fallen leaves and watered by rain, and it suppresses its own weeds. Each year the garden is fuller and lusher than the year before, thanks to my silent partner—nature.

When planning a low-maintenance garden, keep these things in mind:

- *Lawns are labor-intensive ground covers.* They require untold hours of mowing, raking, weeding, fertilizing and watering. This expense is justified when you need some grass to provide a resilient ground cover for walking, sunbathing, badminton or other activities, but it is an extravagance when the lawn is just a decoration, as many are. So maintain only as much lawn as you will really use, and get rid of the rest. My patch of grass is just big enough to hold a blanket and a couple of lawn chairs.

- *Avoid shrubs that require pruning.* Choose plants that grow attractively all by themselves. Don't trim shrubs into rectangular hedges or into cones, balls and other unnatural geometric shapes.

- *Bring color and interest into your garden with flowering trees and shrubs,* not just with labor-intensive annuals and perennials. Also try variegated shrubs and ground covers, handsome rocks, and garden furniture and sculpture.

- *If you do use annual or perennial flowers, plant them sparingly.* Use them to their best effect as small but powerful accents— for example, in the middle of a mass of evergreens.

Even a small woodlot can make a typical yard look like an estate. Removing dead trees and understory plants from a wooded area produces an expansive, parklike effect. Then cultivated ornamental plants can be added to create a woodland garden.

PLANT EVERGREENS AND ORNAMENTAL GRASSES FOR YEAR-ROUND INTEREST

Many estate gardeners maintain interest the hard way—by replacing flowers that have already bloomed with new ones that are about to bloom. This requires lots of time and a large plant budget. It also doesn't solve the problem of seasonal change for those in colder climates: how to cover dull, barren ground during the drab months in spring and fall.

As New England landscape architect Charles Eliot wisely counseled, the solution to one-third of a year of bare ground is evergreens. Plant at least half your garden with evergreen trees, ground covers and shrubs.

Also consider ornamental grasses, which are the natural equivalent of dried arrangements. In late fall and early winter, their tawny tuffets contrast handsomely with snow.

BORROW NEIGHBORING SCENERY TO ENHANCE YOUR OWN PROPERTY

Another efficient way for small-lot owners to simulate a large estate is by "borrowing" scenery that's actually outside the lot's perimeter. Borrowing is the opposite of berming. A berm hides an undesirable view. Borrowing uses a desirable view.

Behind my house are low granite cliffs, a seasonal stream and a majestic wood composed almost entirely of tall white pines. Only a portion of these lovely features are actually on my lot. But as I walk around the yard, my eyes make no such legal distinction. To borrow as much of this beauty as I can, I've made

paths through my yard that take me to the best views.

CULTIVATE WOODLAND GARDENS FOR AN EXTRA DIMENSION

If you have even a tiny woodlot on your land, you can create a woodland garden. A woodland garden gives you so much for so little. Most gardens are two-dimensional: They consist mainly of flowers and low shrubs planted on what landscape designers call the "ground plane," which is the earth "floor" of the garden "room." Woodland gardens, on the other hand, are three-dimensional. They include not only understory plants but also large trees, whose trunks make up the walls and whose canopies compose the ceiling of a massive outdoor room. When you walk in a woodland garden, you walk not only over beauty but, as Lord Byron put it, in beauty.

If you already have a woodlot, you won't have to create a woodland garden; you just have to complete it. First, remove debris and most of the dead trees, both standing and fallen. Then weed out unwanted trees and other plants, including most hardwoods with trunks less than 6 in. or so in diameter. Next, cut some winding paths. Cleaning up and weeding the wood—what I call gardening-by-subtraction—creates a more open, nearly parklike forest.

The final step in creating a woodland garden is gardening-by-addition. Plant shade-tolerant evergreen shrubs, such as rhododendrons and azaleas (*Rhododendron* spp.), mountain laurel (*Kalmia latifolia*), leucothoë (*Leucothoë fontanesiana*) and *Pieris japonica* along the paths. Between the shrubs, plant equally shade-tolerant evergreen ground covers, such as pachysandra (*Pachysandra terminalis*), ivy (*Hedera helix*) and wild ginger (*Asarum canadense*).

"The final step in creating a woodland garden is gardening-by-addition."

When you're done, you'll be surrounded by a private garden that's cool even on warm days; that fertilizes, waters and mulches itself; that's nearly weed-free; and that grows lusher every year.

GET MORE GARDEN FOR LESS MONEY

While the garden I describe should be inexpensive to take care of, it is not necessarily inexpensive to install. That's the bad news. The good news is that there are plenty of ways to stretch your landscaping budget:

- *Buy inexpensive species.* Rhododendrons, for example, are often the least costly broad-leaved evergreen shrubs. Also, their foliage is denser and they often grow faster than mountain laurels or andromedas, so they give you more mass for your money. Another example: You can cover space more cheaply with pachysandra than with any other evergreen ground cover, and it has the added benefit of being the easiest evergreen ground cover to install.

- *Buy small plants instead of large ones.* They're not only cheaper but also a better risk because they transplant more successfully than large plants and, if one dies, your loss is minimal.

- *Buy plants in quantity.* Find a nursery that will give you a discount for buying three dozen rhododendrons or 500 pachysandra plants. For best results, make your request in the winter, before plant retailers place their orders with wholesalers. Also buy plants in late summer or fall, when many are marked down.

- *Free up money for plants by avoiding costly hardscaping.* One client told me he wanted to build several retaining walls (for about $10,000) below some steep grades to hold the soil against erosion. I told him to plant

the slopes with shrubs and ground covers for about $1,000 and to use the $9,000 saved on walls to build and plant berms.

- *Remember that you don't have to create your estate all at once.* You should do only as much as you can afford each year.

- *Consider plants a good investment.* Every dollar spent replacing an unused lawn area with an evergreen ground cover, or screening with berms and shrubs, pays off with less time and money spent on maintenance and with a more beautiful, more private and more valuable property.

Pathways lead visitors to the prettiest views. A path strewn with pine needles winds through the garden to allow glimpses of "borrowed" scenery.

KEITH GELLER

is a residential design-and-build landscape architect based in Seattle, Washington. He teaches a design class at the Center for Urban Horticulture.

Creating Garden Passageways

Sometimes the areas connected by transitional spaces are similar in character. These brick courtyards are similar looking, but they differ in size and function.

GARDENS HAVE THE power to evoke emotion and drama—one area may feel open and spacious; another, cozy and intimate. Yet what I enjoy most about gardens is experiencing the movement from one area to another. It allows me to participate in that garden, whether I created it or not.

Transitional areas, by their very nature, connect two distinct spaces. These spaces may be very similar in character or vary considerably from one another. Whether paths, steps, gates, landings, grade changes, or plantings are used to segue from one garden room to another, such areas should be carefully designed to signal a change in place or experience. Sometimes these transitional spaces themselves are sub-rooms that have a charm and character different from the spaces they are linking.

The tree canopy partially obscures your final destination, creating a sense of mystery.

The table serves as a focal point to draw you along the path.

The surfacing material changes from bark mulch to brick as you make the transition from woodland path to courtyard.

A large, water-filled container marks the entrance to the courtyard.

The narrow, shaded path ends and space opens up, so you know you're in a new place.

START BY DEFINING THE SPACES

No matter how large or small a residential garden, there should be a sequence of experiences equivalent to an approach, an arrival, and an invitation to participate in the garden itself. But to achieve continuous physical movement through a garden, you must first identify the potential outdoor spaces or rooms that surround your home. Clues for defining outdoor rooms are often found by studying the existing conditions of a site. For instance, a wall of your house or an outbuilding may double as the wall of a garden room. Existing trees and shrubs, expanses of lawn, topographical changes, and views also define spaces. Once these outdoor spaces have been identified, you

"The nature of paths is that they connect one place to another and lead to a destination."

False cypress trees frame the entry courtyard.

A gate divides the public and private spaces in the landscape.

Space narrows as you pass from one area to another.

A large container planting marks the entry into a new space.

Change in grade and paving material signals a transition.

can link them so the flow from one area to another is smooth and experiential.

My own garden, which scales a steep hillside, consists of a series of rooms: a small, semi-public room at street level; an entry courtyard near the front door; a small, terraced area for dining; a courtyard garden out back; and an intimate sitting area beneath an arbor near the corner of the lot, just big enough for two people. These areas are connected by a series of paths and steps wending their way through the property, often creating garden rooms of their own.

PATHWAYS LEAD TO A DESTINATION

The nature of paths is that they connect one place to another and lead to a destination. Quite often, the destination is visible at the end of the path or just beyond it in the form of a focal point—perhaps a sculpture, statue, or bench that draws our attention.

In my own garden, a woodland path along the side of the house connects the entry courtyard to the dining area. As I walk along the path, I can see the dining table, slightly obscured by the tree canopy, which lures me to the terrace. This interrupted view actually helps make the arrival more eventful and appealing.

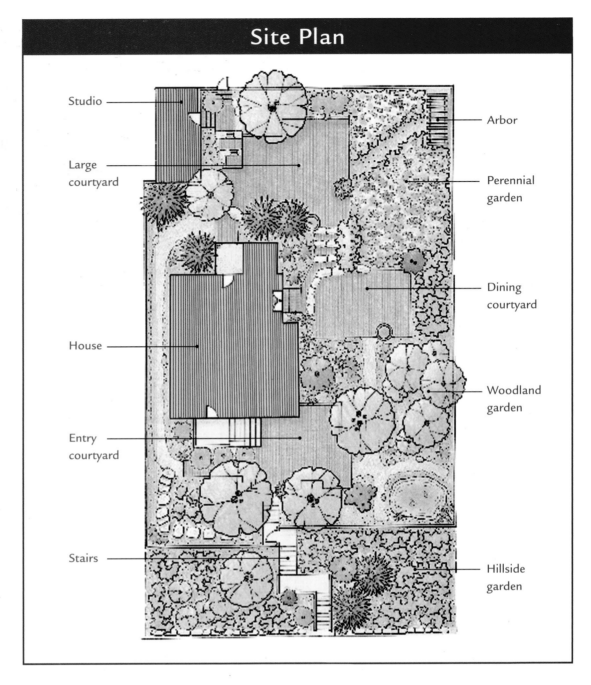

Studio

Large courtyard

House

Entry courtyard

Stairs

Arbor

Perennial garden

Dining courtyard

Woodland garden

Hillside garden

Not far from my terraced courtyard is a small sitting area beneath the arbor. The space between them was the sunniest spot in the garden, so I knew it would be best reserved for perennials. Instead of making a walkway along the edge of a perennial border, I created a narrow path that meanders *through* the border, so the walk becomes a participatory experience, letting you focus on the floral details as you move from one space to another. By adding points of interest between the destinations, I was able to create a greater sense of depth in this garden.

GRADE CHANGES MARK TRANSITIONS

Grade changes indicate that you're entering a new space, so locate your property's natural grade changes and try to incorporate steps in your design. Even a single step can create an effective transition from one space into another; a flight of stairs can be dramatic.

Between the sidewalk and the reception area near my front door, a long stairway ascends the steep hillside. The steps signal that you are leaving the public space and entering a private garden. Steps act much like a pathway through a garden, except that the elevation gain further emphasizes a change in environments.

A less dramatic, but equally important grade change occurs between the small dining area and terraced courtyard. Three broad steps connect the two spaces, as well as provide access to the kitchen door. Because they are made of stone and brick that match the terrace materials, they create a subtle and pleasing transition.

LANDINGS: A PLACE TO PAUSE

The landing just outside your door plays an essential role in creating a transitional space between your home and garden. Because of this, landings—whether a single, broad step or a covered porch—should, ideally, incorporate materials that reflect both the house and the garden. For instance, a porch would most likely be made from the same construction materials as the house, but its posts may be draped in vines. Or, you could use materials for the flooring to provide the garden link.

Landings also provide a place to pause and experience the surrounding landscape. For this reason, landings are sometimes placed throughout the garden. A good example is the landing that I placed at the top of my stairs that lead from the street, where you are forced to pause and look around the garden. On your way up the hillside, there is also another landing where you can catch your breath. On a sunny morning, I often sit here and watch the birds.

PLANTINGS MAKE NATURAL TRANSITIONS

Trees and shrubs are the bones of a garden and, with careful placement, can define the rooms that help make a garden feel inviting. They can also serve as transitional elements. For instance, a tree at the edge of one outdoor space may also mark the entry into another area. I have an elegant, multiple-trunked vine maple (*Acer circinatum*) at the edge of the entry courtyard introducing my woodland garden and path. And two 60-year-old false cypress trees (*Chamaecyparis lawsoniana* 'Allumii') thrive opposite one another at the top of the stairs, marking the transition from the hillside garden to the entry courtyard.

Even a sidewalk can be turned into a garden room with the effective use of transitional elements. Notice how different paving materials are used to signal change and plantings are used to enclose the space.

"Landings also provide a place to pause and experience the surrounding landscape."

"Stepping from my mulched woodland path onto the brick patio, you know at once that you are entering a new space."

This sunny spot doubles as a perennial garden and a participatory garden walk. It leads from the upper courtyard to the secluded seating area beneath an arbor. Along the way, you can touch, smell, and observe the flowers.

Trees planted on either side of this path help mark the transition. The path, which starts at the edge of the open, upper courtyard, travels through a narrow and deeply shaded section of the garden.

Their huge, drooping, multibranched trunks create a fascinating and comforting canopy to pass beneath before approaching the house.

When connecting two open spaces, it is helpful to narrow the passage between them. I used this approach effectively between the two brick terraces.

In addition to the grade change marked by the three broad steps, the garden closes in on this space for a more intimate transition. And the fragrance that fills the air when you brush

against a large rosemary on the way to the upper terrace instantly puts your senses in touch with the garden.

USE STRUCTURES TO SIGNAL AN ENTRANCE

Arches, gates, low fencing, or large containers flanking an entry all help mark a transition. I have used these elements throughout my garden. For example, after climbing the stairs from the street, the front gate marks the transition into a more private space. A small arbor

The landing provides a place to pause and view the garden.

Brick steps link the house and lower courtyard.

An Adirondack chair serves as a focal point, drawing the eye from one courtyard to the next.

Grade changes signal that you're moving from one space to another.

Although the spaces are similar, the narrow passageway divides them.

or arch could be used to similar effect, requiring you to pass through it into the next space. In the backyard, I use a low, split-rail fence to identify the beginning of the perennial garden path as it leads from the large brick terrace. Its rustic construction signals that you are moving into a more informal area.

Throughout the garden, I've also used large containers—sometimes with plantings, and sometimes just filled with water for the birds—to highlight the point at which you move from one area to another. They also serve as focal points, drawing your eye through the garden, encouraging you to explore just a bit farther down the garden path.

A simple change in paving materials can signal a transition. Stepping from my mulched woodland path onto the brick patio, you know at once that you are entering a new space. Whether your transitions are as subtle as the narrowing of a passage or as clear as a gate or arbor, emphasizing passageways is a creative way to highlight the changing moods and experiences in your garden.

RICK DARKE

is a noted horticulturist and former curator of plants for Longwood Gardens. He is author of *The Color Encyclopedia of Ornamental Grasses* and *In Harmony with Nature: Lessons from the Arts and Crafts Garden.*

Celebrating Natural Light
in the Landscape

(LEFT) Placing objects that accentuate light patterns expands a garden's interest. A cedar sculpture frames the rising sun on an October morning.

(INSET) The same sculpture frames the rising moon in early spring.

WHILE COLOR IN NATIVE landscapes ebbs and flows, the cycles of sunlight, moonlight, and starlight create visual drama in every season. Like personal signatures, these cycles vary with each region, providing subtle, but sure, ways of identifying a place.

To celebrate the process and pattern of natural light, my wife, Melinda, and I chose to make it the design theme of our garden. We thought this approach would enhance the year-round intrigue of our landscape and help us stay connected with natural rhythms and ecology. The resulting garden is a daily source of enjoyment and gives us insights into nearby native landscapes.

We found support for our design motif in the writings of two visionary landscape architects—Jens Jensen and O. C. Simonds. In a *Saturday Evening Post* article in 1930, Jensen counted the landscape gardener's raw materials as

"I learned much about natural light in the landscape from a photographic study that I began in 1983."

(RIGHT) Bark catches light. The sunlit peeling bark of a 'Heritage' river birch creates a luminous effect.

(BELOW) The translucency of plants is deepened by changing light. The fruits of a two-winged silverbell glow lime-green in late-October light.

"the contours of the earth, the vegetation that covers it, the changing seasons, the rays of the setting sun and the afterglow, and the light of the moon." In his 1920 book, *Landscape Gardening*, Simonds drew an analogy with the landscape painter's approach to composition, suggesting that the sky is the gardener's canvas, and that the "earth itself, the ocean, mountains, hills, prairies or forests" are seen against this background. He advised gardeners to leave space on this canvas to be filled with "clouds and sunshine, with stars and moonlight."

Simonds' analogy resonated for Melinda and me. We share a longtime interest in the turn-of-the-century Arts and Crafts movement, which celebrated vernacular materials and advocated the pursuit of art in everyday life. "Nature" was considered an ideal source of artistic inspiration. Many landscape painters of this era took their work outdoors, and the drama of natural light often figured prominently in such *plein air* paintings, as they were known.

Likewise, we've aimed for a painterly approach to garden-making. We try to work with our entire "canvas," including both the broad effects and subtle nuances of light.

OBSERVE LIGHT PATTERNS FOR DESIGN INSPIRATION

Melinda and I are horticulturists by profession, and we both first studied the natural sciences and ecology. This background influences the way we relate to landscapes and gardening.

I learned much about natural light in the landscape from a photographic study that I began in 1983, when my daily commute to work at Longwood Gardens took me over a bridge crossing the Red Clay Creek. Typical of the eastern Pennsylvania landscape, this wood-

land creek flows past stately tulip trees and beeches, and under majestically arching sycamores.

I photographed from the same spot almost daily the first year, often in the morning, during lunch, and on the way home in the evening. I recorded the date and time of each photograph and jotted quick observations about the weather, the sunlight, and the shadows. I sometimes noted what I considered to be the mood of the landscape, as well as my own mood.

In time, I became attuned to qualities of light that characterized each time of day, each month, and each season. I came to appreciate the glow of golden sunbeams through new beech leaves in mid-May and the subtle morning light in January illuminating hoarfrost on tawny seed heads. This study also taught me

(ABOVE) The morning sun illuminates ice-covered woodlands in this view from the author's garden to an adjacent preserve. This scene can be enjoyed from indoors as well.

(LEFT) Connecting the house to the garden gives a feeling of harmony. The soft glow of a mica lampshade echoes the winter light shining through the bark of a 'Heritage' river birch.

Great Plants for Catching Light

The following plants are especially valuable for their translucent flowers, foliage, or seed heads. All are hardy in Zones 5 to 8; some are hardier or more heat-tolerant.

TREES & SHRUBS

American beech (*Fagus grandifolia*)
Black gum (*Nyssa sylvatica*)
Bottlebrush buckeye (*Aesculus parviflora*)
Common witch hazel (*Hamamelis virginiana*)
Cutleaf smooth sumac (*Rhus glabra* 'Laciniata')
Cutleaf staghorn sumac (*Rhus typhina* 'Laciniata')
Dwarf fothergilla (*Fothergilla gardenii*)
'Forest Pansy' redbud (*Cercis canadensis* 'Forest Pansy')
Katsura tree (*Cercidiphyllum japonicum*)
Maple-leaved viburnum (*Viburnum acerifolium*)
Mountain silverbell (*Halesia tetraptera* var. *monticola*)
Pagoda dogwood (*Cornus alternifolia*)
River birch (*Betula nigra*)
Sassafras (*Sassafras albidum*)
Sorrel tree (*Oxydendrum arboreum*)
Two-winged silverbell (*Halesia diptera* var. *magniflora*)
Umbrella tree (*Magnolia tripetala*)

HERBACEOUS PERENNIALS

Black snakeroot (*Cimicifuga racemosa*)
'The Blues' little bluestem (*Schizachyrium scoparium* 'The Blues')
Broom-sedge (*Andropogon virginicus*)
'Cloud Nine' switch grass (*Panicum virgatum* 'Cloud Nine')
'Heavy Metal' switch grass (*Panicum virgatum* 'Heavy Metal')
'Montrose Ruby' alum root (*Heuchera* 'Montrose Ruby')
Prairie dock (*Silphium terebinthinaceum*)
Purple lovegrass (*Eragrostis spectabilis*)
Purpletop (*Tridens flavus*)
'Sioux Blue' Indian grass (*Sorghastrum nutans* 'Sioux Blue')
Switch grass (*Panicum virgatum*)
Threadleaf bluestar (*Amsonia hubrichtii*)
Wherry's foam flower (*Tiarella wherryi*)
White wood aster (*Aster divaricatus*)
Wild oats (*Chasmanthium latifolium*)

---

the value of a notebook and camera as tools to learn about landscape. My notes and images are far more revealing of pattern and process than memory alone could be.

STUDY LIGHT ON YOUR SITE FROM MANY VANTAGE POINTS

Melinda and I always consider both indoor and outdoor views as we design the garden. We observe our own patterns of activity, so that we can organize views around our most-frequented places or paths. We often stroll the garden mornings and evenings, and rarely miss a full moon. On these relaxing walks we notice patterns of light and how we might accentuate them. I usually carry my camera to record intriguing views or events in the garden, and reviewing these photos often inspires our designs.

My creek study also taught me that routine immersion in a landscape gives the best under-standing and appreciation of its detail and merits. This supported our belief that the home should be intimately connected with the garden.

We're fortunate to live near a large wood-land preserve. Our house had large windows on the south side with views of an adjacent historic farm and the preserve beyond. Over the years, the house has been enlarged and modified so that the garden is readily visible from most rooms.

"Natural lighting can often render foliage more striking than flowers."

LOOK FOR PLANTS THAT ARE ENHANCED BY NATURAL LIGHT

My interest in ornamental grasses also taught me much about natural light. I was first drawn to the subtle beauty of grasses two decades ago. Though they lack colorful flowers, they add structure with their distinctive lines and shapes, and their luminosity lasts from season to season. Grasses depend on natural backlighting or sidelighting for dramatic presence. I enhance these translucent effects by designing plantings that place grasses between the sun and the intended viewing point.

We have designed much of the garden to accentuate light patterns. Tall trees block the western horizon, but we can watch the sun and moon come up over the eastern rise and flood the garden with their glow. One border is designed on an axis with these rising spheres, planted with mountain silverbells (*Halesia tetraptera* var. *monticola*), two-winged silverbells (*Halesia diptera* var. *magniflora*), and dwarf fothergillas (*Fothergilla gardenii*). In spring, the delicate parts of these white-flowered species glow in either sunlight or moonlight. In autumn, the golden foliage of the silverbells and the rich reds of the fothergilla leaves are especially vibrant in morning and midday light. The winged fruits of the silverbells last through winter, with each species enhanced by winter's light.

Natural lighting can often render foliage more striking than flowers. I once came upon a stand of umbrella trees (*Magnolia tripetala*) in a Virginia forest late in the day when their 30-in. leaf clusters glowed honey-green in the fading light. I photographed it and resolved to reproduce this effect in the garden someday. We eventually realized we had the perfect opportunity under a tall oak off the south side of the house. The high shade of the oak pro-

Combine plants to heighten the effects of light. Here, a sidelit golden river of thread-leaf blue-star flows between *Sedum* 'Matrona' and *Viburnum nudum* Winterthur'.

The author and his wife stroll their garden in early morning to enjoy the play of light. These walks often inspire future garden ideas.

Natural lighting creates dramatic interplay. Here, the mid-October sun illuminates the glass panes of a sculpture and the seed heads of 'Sioux Blue' Indian grass.

vides the right cultural conditions for two umbrella trees. In morning, then in late afternoon, the sun's rays dramatically light the huge leaves from the side, providing a stunning display visible from inside.

Sometimes a garden effect plays off something indoors. A drift of river birches (*Betula nigra* 'Heritage') flows near the edge of our dining porch. On winter mornings, the sun's low-angled rays cause the birches' peeling bark to gleam a warm orange-red, mirroring the light from the mica shade of a hammered-copper lamp on a table on the porch.

ENHANCE THE EFFECTS OF LIGHT WITH SCULPTURAL OBJECTS

Some of our greatest enjoyment of natural light has resulted from placing two sculptures in the garden. Both were designed to reveal and celebrate the patterns of the sun and moon.

The first sculpture was inspired by a scene in a nearby preserve. A double-trunked tulip tree had fallen across another with three trunks, lodging at a steep angle with the trunks pointing toward the sky. This bit of natural sculpture was most appealing when silhouetted against autumn sunsets. We decided to emulate this on our property by producing a similar silhouette and drawing attention to the rising sun and moon.

We made posts from dead red cedars (*Juniperus virginiana*) we found still standing in the fence-row nearby and built a simple structure of posts radiating from two center points, one on the ground and one at the apex, with only gravity holding them together. This sculptural device keenly reveals the cycles of sun, moon, and seasons. The angles formed by the cedar posts frame the rising sun and moon from different vantage points throughout the year.

We created our second sculpture from sections of copper-sheathed window sash that originally served as vents at the top of Longwood Gardens' main conservatory. We'd purchased these following a restoration of the glasshouse.

It took a while to find an ideal site. We knew the time-etched glass panes would be perfect for capturing glancing sunrays and

"We knew the time-etched glass panes would be perfect for capturing glancing sunrays and moonbeams."

moonbeams, but we wanted to position our sculpture for the most impact from indoors. We tested various locations before settling on a position in our meadow garden directly in line with our bedroom view. This put the sculpture nearly parallel to the arc of the sun and the moon, exposing the glass panes to the greatest natural sidelighting and backlighting, especially in colder months when we were likely to view the piece from inside. I next sketched numerous ways in which we might arrange the sash sections and we finally chose a stepped configuration reminiscent of skyscrapers. We christened our creation the "Meadow Metropolis."

The celebration of natural light has proved a truly satisfying basis for our garden designs, producing a exciting landscape rich with change and seasonal dynamics. It also teaches us to set our gaze high and wide, and to make the fullest use of our landscape canvas. Most significantly, it makes us intimately aware of the rhythms and rituals of our regional woodlands—those subtle details that reveal the spirit of a place.

FRONT YARD
IDEAS

3

WHY IS IT THAT most gardens are relegated to the backyard and most front yards are bland, at best? Why not make a good first impression and create a little curb appeal? Who knows, maybe your neighbors will even take your cue and spruce up their own front yards.

Front yard plantings need not be restricted to overgrown evergreens. Instead, turn your front yard into a cottage garden, a natural site that attracts birds and butterflies, or an engaging entry garden. Guests will linger longer, and feel welcome as they approach your front door.

Keep a few practical matters in mind, too. You want visitors to reach your home safely and easily, without tripping on uneven walks or being snagged by over-zealous plantings. Our designers will offer some useful tips, as well as some innovative ideas for creating a welcoming entry.

BARBARA BLOSSOM ASHMUN

is a garden designer, writer, consultant, and author of several books, including *Garden Retreats* and *The Garden Design Primer*. She is a contributing editor for *Fine Gardening*.

Design
a Welcoming
Entrance

Container plantings and a flowering vine frame the front door, signaling a place of entry.

THE FRONT ENTRY is the most frequently traveled space in a garden, where a lasting first impression is formed even before the doorbell is rung. Sometimes, though, there's such a jumble of paths that you can't find the front door. Or you get lost in a jungle of plants, snagged by rose thorns, or drenched by wet, overhanging foliage. Chances are, you've slid on slippery bricks, tromped through mud, or tripped on uneven paving when visiting someone. Of course, I think that the saddest entries of all are those with only a few lonely evergreens growing in a sea of bleak barkdust.

Yet with just a little attention to path design and planting, it's easy to create a clear sense of direction and a warm sense of welcome. The entry is a passageway from the street to your home, as well as a prelude to your garden. It is a kind of foyer—a place to greet your guests, to establish a hospitable mood, and to give them a taste of your garden.

ENCLOSURES MAKE ENTRIES FEEL INTIMATE

Although front entries are usually not as secluded as backyards, they can be a lot more intimate than the typical expanse of lawn open to the road. The degree of privacy that you create will depend on how much space you have. On a large lot with an ample backyard, privacy in the entry garden may be less critical than in a small city garden where every inch is precious. You may even want to enclose your entry, transforming it into a courtyard for sitting and dining.

Any degree of enclosure increases the intimacy. A grove of trees that branch low on the trunk or a grouping of shrubs can screen out the road while offering seasonal beauty. Lowering the ceiling helps too—the canopy of a single tree may be enough to suggest a roof between sky and earth, to link the structural element of your home to green, growing plants.

For more well-defined boundaries, build a wall or fence, or plant an evergreen hedge to frame your entry garden. Depending on how much separation is desired, you may choose a solid wall of stone, brick, or boards, or a partly open one of pickets or wrought iron. A low stone wall can enclose the entry visually, yet also invite the neighbors to sit and visit awhile.

Whether your entry is enclosed or mostly open to the street, an inviting gate or vine-covered arbor makes a welcoming feature for guests to pass through, reminding them that they are entering new, more personal territory with delightful surprises ahead.

A fence encloses this garden, creating a sense of intimacy, while a vine-covered arbor marks the entrance.

DRESS UP THE FRONT DOOR

Your guests should be able to spot the front door without any hesitation, and the door itself, with surrounding greenery, should be attractive. The architecture of your home determines the scale and grandeur of the entry area, but the addition of a few vines or container plantings can enhance even the most modest entry.

My ranch-style home is a good example. It was as plain as packaged bread until a generous friend built an arbor just forward of the small porch to frame the front door and give it more importance. Now covered with maroon *Clematis* 'Madame Julia Correvon' and fragrant white jasmine (*Jasminum officinale*), the arbor transforms the house into a country cottage. Even without an arbor, it is possible to train a vine up and over the front door to embellish the architecture.

Some day I hope to pave a bigger landing at the base of the porch so that more containers filled with colorful annuals can greet my visitors as they arrive. Pots are a great opportunity for seasonal displays of color that can be changed and refreshed for renewed interest with just a little effort. An ample landing also gives us a chance to take a breath and shift gears before leaving the outside world and entering the private shelter of a home.

PATHS ARE A PRACTICAL MATTER

A clear path unmistakably points the way to the front door. It should be easy on the eyes and feet. This is not a place for stepping stones, uneven cobbles, or wood that becomes slippery when wet. Exposed aggregate textured with small pebbles makes for good traction, especially in wet weather. One day, I hope to replace my mundane concrete sidewalk with a pebble mosaic path to the front door. Similar to exposed aggregate, but more artfully ornamental, pebble mosaic also adds traction underfoot.

Make your path wide enough for two people to walk side by side, leaving a little extra space so visitors don't have to brush against wet or prickly shrubs. An established concrete path can be widened by adding brick trim laid perpendicular to the sidewalk. This not only widens the path, but dresses it up as well.

No matter which materials you choose—whether stone, concrete, brick, or even crushed stone—make your path level and easy to navigate. If there are steps or stairs, make sure they are safe. Broad steps with low risers make climbing easier, and handrails are recommended along staircases. Stairs themselves can be art objects when faced with stone or other decorative materials.

If at all possible, instead of aiming the path straight for the front door, let it wend its way through the entry garden more gradually, so that your guests travel slowly and luxuriously, enjoying glimpses of beautiful plants and breathing in enticing fragrances. Welcome visitors to your home with clove-scented cottage pinks (*Dianthus plumarius*) or lavender planted along the edges of the walkway. Let the path flow beneath the leafy canopy of a Japanese snowbell (*Styrax japonicus*), so visitors can enjoy a view up into the dangling white flowers.

"An inviting gate or vine-covered arbor makes a welcoming feature for guests to pass through."

Curved paths are more interesting than straight ones, especially when softened with plantings.

PLANTINGS PROVIDE PERSONALITY

Interesting evergreens keep an entry attractive at all seasons, especially if you combine plants with diverse textures, shapes, and foliage colors. Fine-textured conifers such as hinoki cypress (*Chamaecyparis obtusa*) and Himalayan pine (*Pinus wallichiana*) contrast nicely with the bolder foliage of broad-leaved evergreens such as camellia, rhododendron, or evergreen magnolia (*Magnolia grandiflora*). Picture the vast hand-shaped leaves of Japanese aralia (*Fatsia japonica*) against the delicate foliage of evergreen huckleberry

> *"Gold, silver, and variegated leaves will make your entry colorful without a single flower in bloom."*

(*Vaccinium ovatum*) or boxleaf honeysuckle (*Lonicera nitida*). *Rhododendron* 'Daphnoides' has beautifully scalloped leaves, while the foliage of *Rhododendron williamsianum* is heart-shaped. Camellia and sweet box (*Sarcococca confusa*, *S. ruscifolia*, and *S. hookeriana* var. *humilis*) are so shiny they might have been lacquered. Heavenly bamboo (*Nandina domestica*), on the other hand, has a matte finish, more like a grass. And the leaves of 'Allegheny' viburnum (*Viburnum* × *rhytido-phylloides* 'Allegheny') are so marvelously embossed that they thrill me every time I encounter them.

Gold, silver, and variegated leaves will make your entry colorful without a single flower in bloom. For the cooling effect of felted silver, try *Senecio greyii* or *Phlomis fruticosa*. The leathery, khaki leaves of *Elaeagnus pungens* 'Maculata' are brightly splashed with gold, while 'Sundance' Mexican orange (*Choisya ternata* 'Sundance') flaunts yellow leaves in a

A small, deciduous tree offers shade in summer and lets sunlight shine in during winter. It also serves as a focal point from indoors.

beautiful trifoliate pattern. Variegated leaves abound: try 'Emerald Gaiety' wintercreeper (*Euonymus fortunei* 'Emerald Gaiety') between larger shrubs or try variegated boxwood (*Buxus sempervirens* 'Argenteovariegata') to anchor a bed.

Fragrant plants can be especially enchanting. Include as many as possible to lift your spirits year-round. The earliest scents of winter-blooming sweet box and pink winter daphne (*Daphne odora*) will transform the bleakest winter day. Both sweet box and daphne are evergreen, as is the spring-blooming *Osmanthus delavayi*, with handsome, dark leaves and pure-white flowers.

I also rely on a few evergreen perennials to frame the edges of entry beds and embellish them with long-lasting color. My all time favorite for shade is lenten rose (*Helleborus orientalis*) with handsome, palmate leaves and

nodding, winter flowers in shades of pink and cream. *Helleborus foetidus* 'Wester Flisk', named for the old Scottish rectory where it first appeared, draws admiring glances year-round. Its pinwheel-shaped leaves have wine-colored tints that make everyone stop for a second look. The cabbagy leaves of *Bergenia ciliata* are all the more interesting for their downy coating of fine hair. In sun or shade, bergenia foliage gives some oomph to the edge of a border. Equally substantial for shade or partial shade, *Geranium macrorrhizum* provides nicely lobed leaves and a brilliant topping of magenta flowers. It spreads quickly but is easily thinned out as needed.

By adding a few deciduous trees, shrubs, and vines, as well as herbaceous perennials that die down in winter, you will give your entry garden the refreshing element of seasonal change. Each spring I look forward to the unfurling of the round, burgundy leaves of 'Royal Purple' smoke tree (*Cotinus coggygria* 'Royal Purple'). When the small stems of lily-of-the-valley (*Convallaria majalis*) fill with tiny, fragrant, white bells, my heart lifts. What greater joy than watching blue lungwort (*Pulmonaria* 'Roy Davidson') bloom in harmony with yellow daffodils? And leave some room to tuck in a handful of white 'Casa Blanca' lilies (*Lilium* 'Casa Blanca') to perfume the summer garden, or a drift of Kaffir lilies (*Schizostylis coccinea*) so that their coral flowers may glow in autumn. Underplant shrubs with pools of magenta winter-blooming cyclamen (*Cyclamen coum*) and white snowdrops (*Galanthus nivalis*) so that not an inch of ground is wasted. Make your entry a cornucopia of color, texture, and fragrance.

HIDE THE FOUNDATION, NOT THE WINDOWS

Both homes I've lived in were darkened by overgrown rhododendrons and Japanese pieris (*Pieris japonica*) growing smack up against the windows. Out they came, and off they went to other gardens where they would serve as hedges. Avoid these predictable problems by softening the foundation with low-growing evergreens, or at least ones that can be easily pruned to keep their heights in check. Dwarf forms of mountain laurel (*Kalmia latifolia*), *Camellia sasanqua*, and evergreen huckleberry (*Vaccinium ovatum*) are just a few of the many choices available.

Where you need some protection from the sun, a deciduous tree with an interesting trunk and branching pattern makes an appealing focal point near a window, letting in winter light while providing some shade in summer. Just remember to choose deep-rooted trees near the foundation of the house so the ground beneath them will be friendlier to perennials and ground covers.

In an entry garden, you must consider the relationship of plants to the house. If chosen carefully, trees and shrubs will enhance the architecture and their sizes and shapes will be in pleasing proportion to the structural elements. It is especially important to plant trees or shrubs to camouflage the sharp vertical lines of house corners and downspouts and to unite the home and garden. A house all by itself looms large, isolated from the surrounding larger landscape. However, softened by trees and foundation plantings, it joins and blends more naturally with its environment. Keep in mind the ultimate sizes of trees so that they don't grow into the gutters or overhang the roofline. Take into consideration the mature size of a tree's canopy and plant it far enough from the house so that it may gracefully spread its branches.

Throughout the year, your entry garden can be a place of delight, anchored by plenty of evergreens for permanent greenery and embellished with more fleeting flowers to celebrate the unique joy of each season. Let it be a welcoming haven for those who dwell within and all who arrive to visit.

"A deciduous tree with an interesting trunk and branching pattern makes an appealing focal point near a window."

An informal planting design—with no perceptible geometric structure—complements the informality of this house.

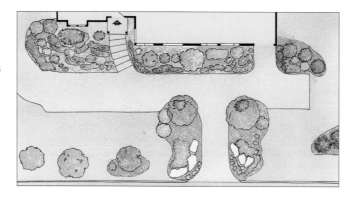

The essential forms of a house and plants can be viewed as interrelated, abstract shapes. Here, a single, cone-shaped conifer rising above the roof eave counterbalances the rectangular mass of the chimney to its right.

Spreading and low-growing foundation plantings reinforce the sweeping lines of this contemporary home and complement the architecture. Stately trees create a pleasing visual frame around the horizontal house.

TODD PHILLIPPI

is an architect, planner, and landscape/garden designer. His gardens are on tour periodically, and he frequently lectures on garden design and ornamental horticulture.

The Fundamentals of
Foundation
Plantings

A group of tall conifers provides a visual endpoint to the house's long, horizontal lines.

IT WAS LOVE and frustration that propelled me into landscape design. My love of gardening is a legacy from my grandparents. My frustration came about as a practicing architect when I observed many landscape plantings that were insensitive to a site's natural features, conflicted with architectural designs, or showcased only a limited repertoire of plants, often incorrectly placed on a site.

I decided to incorporate my knowledge and love of gardening into my architectural work. At first, I experimented with garden design at my home in Philadelphia, and eventually pursued formal training in horticulture. The focus of my work has since shifted to what I call "integrated design"—where a building, site layout, and plantings are designed as a unified entity. Perhaps the most visible aspect of this concept is the design of foundation plantings—the trees, shrubs, vines, grasses, and ground covers

Fundamentally Formal

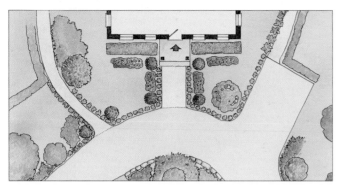

This site plan depicts a predominantly symmetrical design that becomes slightly asymmetrical as it moves away from the house.

The strong horizontal forms of clipped hedges below windows anchor this tall house to the ground. Rounded and triangular plants balance the house's rectangular shape.

A tall conifer is placed so that the corner of the house points to it and there is enough space for its mature growth.

The symmetry of the author's formal-styled home is reinforced by a symmetrical planting design close to the entry, and in the center mound in the foreground.

around a house that create a transition from the built environment to the terrain of the earth.

Foundation plants help to frame a house and anchor it to the site. With imaginative and harmonious planting schemes, the front yard of any home can become a dynamic garden space to be enjoyed rather than merely a static view to be observed.

When plantings are unified with a home, they create more than an attractive picture. They convey a welcoming impression to visitors, and an air of permanence and harmony.

WORK WITH EXISTING ELEMENTS IN THE SITE

A front garden is usually created within the framework of existing architectural and landscape features. To design foundation plantings that are appropriate for a house and its site, I begin by evaluating these elements. They include driveways, walks, streets, large trees, adjacent woodlands, fences, and hedges as well as the house itself. I also look for any areas that are undefined, such as an expanse of lawn on the side of the house that runs into a neighboring property. These open spaces might be ideal areas for new plantings.

Because of their scale, any large trees will be important aspects of a planting design. I always assess their impact and try to determine what other plants might be added for balance, or to strengthen the visual framework of the site. Likewise, an existing row of trees or shrubs might provide a sense of enclosure along a street or driveway. However, rather than completely cutting off the yard from the street, I like to create well-placed views from the street and openings to entice visitors to enter and enjoy the garden space.

Since the house is the single largest element I'm working with, I examine it closely for cues

An informal espalier covers an exterior wall while preserving the window views.

and inspiration. First, I try to define the architectural style of the house, such as Georgian, Colonial, Tudor, or contemporary. Since many homes combine elements of more than one style, I look for the most prominent features—such as gabled roof ends, a bay window, or an entrance porch—and the symmetry or asymmetry of doors and windows.

I also determine whether the shape of the house appears predominantly vertical or horizontal, and whether the general style is formal or informal. A formal house is balanced, usually having a centered front door with an equal number of windows on each side. An informal house will usually have windows and doors that are off-center.

The style of a house often suggests a similar theme for the plantings. Formal garden styles are exactly that. They have a strong, perceptible, geometric form, and are usually symmetrical. In contrast, informal garden styles will not have a perceptible geometric form.

"I like to create well-placed views from the street and openings to entice visitors to enter and enjoy the garden space."

A weeping English yew (*Taxus baccata* 'Repandens') spreads horizontally beneath a window without shearing.

REPEAT OR CONTRAST ARCHITECTURAL LINES

When choosing foundation plants, I consider how their forms can reinforce architectural lines. Narrow trees or tall grasses accentuate the height of the house and echo vertical elements such as chimneys and turrets. Horizontal lines of contemporary homes are reinforced by spreading and weeping trees or low-growing shrubs. The reinforcing lines will complement rather than compete with a house's architecture. On the other hand, several tall conifers in front of a long, one-story house would interrupt its horizontal shape.

By contrast, plantings can also balance architectural forms. Placing a tall conical tree at the corner of a ranch-style house will visually raise its height and give an endpoint to its horizontal lines. Likewise, spreading trees and low shrub masses can balance a house's strong vertical lines and make it appear more grounded. In this case, it's important to avoid simply covering the bottom of the house with shrubs, which can create overpowering horizontal masses that look like skirting.

When planting shrubs beneath windows, and working with informal or semiformal design styles, I look for plants with natural, horizontal growth habits. This will diminish the temptation to shear shrubs into flat-topped or meatball shapes. One of my favorite shrubs with which to create a horizontal effect is weeping English yew (*Taxus baccata* 'Repandens'). Combined with a low ground cover, it will weep and spread for years while retaining its natural, horizontal form.

PRESERVE VIEWS OF KEY ARCHITECTURAL FEATURES

Another principle I use in designing with foundation plantings is to preserve clear views of key architectural features, such as windows, doors, and corners. Many homes have a focal point, such as a two-story arched window. Since the eye is naturally drawn to this part of the house, it becomes a tempting place for a specimen tree such as a weeping Higan cherry (*Prunus subhirtella* 'Pendula'). However, a more effective strategy is to balance the focal point on the house with one in the landscape. If the window is tall and toward the right, I would plant a tree toward the left and away from the house approximately the distance from the ground to the middle of the window.

When placing plantings around an entranceway, I take my cues from the door and mantle. Formal doors with traditionally styled mantles or porticos (small porches at entrances) suggest symmetrical treatment, so I match plants on each side of the entrance. To create a more naturalistic garden around a formal house, plantings can gradually become more informal a short distance from the front door. Modern door styles, such as those with a single glass panel on one side, usually look best

"Spreading trees and low shrub masses can balance a house's strong vertical lines."

A Few Recommended Foundation Plants

NAME		COLOR AND FORM	COMMENTS
TREES			
Japanese maple (*Acer palmatum* cvs.)		Billowy specimen plant in various shades of red and green	Softens structural lines; grow in full sun; Zones 5 to 8
Lawson's false cypress (*Chamaecyparis lawsoniana* 'Columnaris')		A soft and feathery, but dense, blue-toned evergreen	Vertical accent plant; ideal for narrow spaces; grow in full sun; Zones 5 to 7
Weeping Nootka cypress (*Chamaecyparis nootkatensis* 'Pendula')		Dark evergreen with weeping branches; dense or open forms	Dense form more graceful and versatile; grow in full sun; Zones 4 to 7
Chinese dogwood (*Cornus kousa* var. *chinensis*)		White spring flowers and red fall color; low-branched form is best	Horizontal mass can balance house size; grow in partial shade; Zones 5 to 8
Globe Colorado blue spruce (*Picea pungens* 'Glauca Glabosa')		Compact, slow-growing, bluish-white; broad, pyramid-shaped	Good foundation plant; grow in sun to keep blue and dense; Zones 2 to 7
'Capital' Callery pear (*Pyrus calleryana* 'Capital')		Glossy, dark-green leaves that turn copper in fall	Use for narrow espalier or to emphasize height; grow in full sun; Zones 5 to 8
Weeping Canadian hemlock (*Tsuga canadensis* 'Pendula')		Olive-colored evergreen with fine, evenly layered branching	Horizontal accent plant; grow in full sun; Zones 4 to 7
SHRUBS			
Dwarf English boxwood (*Buxus sempervirens* 'Suffruticosa')		Slow-growing plant with glossy, dark-green leaves; tight form	Use for symmetrical hedging; needs partial shade; Zones 5 to 8
Variegated yellow-twig dogwood (*Cornus sericia* 'Silver-n-Gold')		Large, white-edged foliage; arching, yellow stems in winter	Use with informal houses; grow in full to part sun; Zones 2 to 7
Dwarf Japanese pieris (*Pieris japonica* 'Compacta')		Glossy, green foliage with white, drooping flower bracts in spring	Good for flanking formal entrances facing north or east; grow in part sun to shade; Zones 5 to 8
'Mohave' firethorn (*Pyracantha* 'Mohave')		Lustrous, dark-green foliage with heavy, red-orange fruit in fall	For informal espalier or hedge; grow in full sun; Zones 6 to 9
Fairy rose (*Rosa* 'The Fairy')		Masses of soft-pink flowers on low-growing hedgelike shrub	Good, easy-care shrub rose for any garden style; grow in full sun; Zones 3 to 8
PERENNIALS AND GRASSES			
Astilbe (*Astilbe* spp.)		Soft flower plumes in many hues with wispy, fernlike foliage	For adding color to dark corners; grows best in partial shade; Zones 4 to 8
'Stella D'Oro' daylily (*Hemerocallis* 'Stella D'Oro')		Dense tufts of grassy foliage with long-blooming yellow flowers	Use in groups to soften informal edges; grow in full sun; Zones 4 to 8
Hosta (*Hosta* spp.)		Mounding plant in a wide range of textures, sizes, and colors	Versatile edging or contrast plants; grow in partial sun and shade; Zones 3 to 9
'Big Blue' lilyturf (*Liriope muscari* 'Big Blue')		Thick, low, evergreen, grasslike plant with purple flower spikes	Use as edging for walkways; grow in sun or shade; Zones 6 to 10
Japanese silvergrass (*Miscanthus sinensis* 'Morning Light')		Wispy, gray-green mounds of grassy foliage	Lends informal elegance to border areas; grow in full sun; Zones 5 to 10
Japanese forest grass (*Hakonechloa macra* 'Aureola')		Rivers of gold and green strands that ripple with the wind	Use with contemporary homes; grows best in shady areas; Zones 5 to 9

Ruddy-red tones in the shutters are repeated in the russet-colored blooms of *Sedum* 'Autumn Joy'. Fine-leaved plants provide contrast to the rugged texture of stonework.

with asymmetrical plantings. To emphasize the doorway, I'll often group trees and other plantings so they taper down toward such an entrance.

Corners are also important since they define the outline of a house. Often this definition is concealed by plants, such as cone-shaped conifers acting like bookends. If trees or shrubs are needed there to accentuate the house, I place them slightly farther away and let the corner of the house "point" to them. I

plan the exact planting distance so there will be enough space even after the plants have matured.

As with corners, an expansive wall area without windows seems to invite the placement of a tree. Again, I would plant the tree far enough away from the house so that it won't grow into the roof and then appear lopsided as it matures. I also consider alternatives, such as an espalier, or a shrub, such as firethorn (*Pyracantha* spp.), that will grow flat against a wall.

FOLIAGE AND FLOWERS ENHANCE HOUSE DETAILS

As finishing touches, I select plants with foliage or flowers to accent the colors and textures of a house. Russet-colored *Sedum*

"Even entry walks and steps can wed the house to the garden through the use of harmonious or accentuating materials."

'Autumn Joy' can repeat the ruddy-red of a home's shutters. Similarly, a mass of white astilbe along a driveway can reinforce white trim or siding. Fine-leaved plants, such as English boxwood (*Buxus sempervirens* 'Suffruticosa') and periwinkle (*Vinca minor*), provide welcome contrast to a bold fieldstone structure.

Ground covers and hardscaping can further meld a house with its site. Mulches of colored gravel or coarse bark can complement house colors and textures, while a low stone retaining wall can repeat the surface of a house's exterior. Even entry walks and steps can wed the house to the garden through the use of harmonious or accentuating materials. A russet-toned brick walkway can reiterate similar colors in the house exterior and plantings.

As a general rule, I try to keep the plantings from overshadowing the house, and vice versa. When a design is successful, neither would look complete without the other.

Make a Cut-and-Paste Planting Plan on Paper

Testing a planting plan on paper before breaking ground or buying plants can save time, money, and aggravation. I recommend a simple, inexpensive technique for visualizing how a combination of foundation plants will look next to your house. All you need is a photograph of your house; plant pictures from magazines, catalogs, or books; removable tape or rubber cement; scissors; white paper; tracing paper; colored pencils or markers; and access to a photocopier.

First, photograph your house from a distance that includes the garden area you wish to develop. Enlarge the photograph to at least 8½ by 14 inches. A black-and-white photocopied enlargement works well.

Next, locate pictures of plants you are considering for your landscape. Photocopy these pictures, trim around the edges of the plants, and paste them onto sheets of plain, white paper. Then make more photocopies, enlarging or reducing the pictures as needed until the plants are in scale with the photo of your house. A front door is about 6 feet tall, so you can use this figure for establishing scale. I like to make my plants the size they will be at maturity, so that I can see how much room to allow for them in my plan.

Next, position the photocopied plants on the enlargement of your house, using removable tape or rubber cement so you can reposition them as needed. To create a three-dimensional effect, make plants in the foreground slightly larger than those next to the house.

Finally, cover your layered photocopy with a sheet of tracing paper and trace the outline of your house with its new front-yard plantings, which you can color with pencils or markers if you wish. Your customized plan will be an invaluable tool when you shop for plants and again later when you put them in the ground.

BARBARA BLOSSOM ASHMUN

is a garden designer, writer, consultant, and author of several books, including *Garden Retreats* and *The Garden Design Primer*. She is a contributing editor for *Fine Gardening*.

The Enclosed Entry Garden

Bring privacy and intimacy right to the front door. Walls, a ceiling and a floor can make the entry garden an extension of a home's interior. Plantings in front of a fence or over a gate reinforce this sense of privacy.

REMEMBER THE OLD-FASHIONED parlor, full of fancy furniture, that was reserved for special company, its seats rarely rumpled by people? A lot of entry gardens are like those parlors—public spaces made for show rather than use. As a garden designer, my first job when consulting with homeowners is to help design or redesign the entry garden. My goal is to make it a useful, enjoyable space for the family rather than for the mailman or passersby.

Many front yards are right on the road, exposed to traffic, unsightly views and the curiosity of pedestrians. Almost every gardener I know would prefer a private front yard, yet tradition stops them from having the desired separation from the public. At the same time, living space has become increasingly precious as builders cram more and bigger houses onto smaller lots. As the size of the back yard shrinks, so does the outdoor space homeowners have in which to entertain, dine and garden peacefully.

By enclosing the entry to make it a private garden room, many benefits result. You can extend your home's living space to relax as you please. You can salvage valuable sunny exposure for a private place to grow flowers, vegetables or fruit. You can create views to enjoy from inside your house. The enclosing walls of your garden will not only look beautiful, but they will also screen out unsightly areas and reduce road noise, and they can serve as a backdrop for plants.

An enclosed entry garden is like a room because you can think about it as having the elements of a room in your home—walls, a ceiling and a floor. And you can fashion garden rooms in diverse ways to suit your style of living and to complement your home's architecture.

WALLS FOR ENCLOSURE

My first task with clients is selecting the walls. Plants, fences or masonry can form a garden wall and each material has its own set of advantages and disadvantages. Plants offer the benefit of foliage and flowers or berries, depending on the specific varieties chosen, but they generally occupy more space than a fence or wall and require more upkeep. Plants often outreach their bounds, so they will need pruning. Still, the beauty of a living hedge or shrub border is appealing, especially if the homeowner has enough time for maintenance or can afford to hire help.

Hedges occupy less space than looser shrub borders, and they give a crisp, formal appearance to the garden. But for complete privacy, evergreens are a must. I prefer hedges made of needled evergreens—their fine texture creates

just the right backdrop for the showier border shrubs and perennials. Arborvitae (*Thuja occidentalis*), yews (*Taxus baccata* and *Taxus × media*), incense cedar (*Calocedrus decurrens*) and Canadian hemlock (*Tsuga canadensis*) are excellent choices in my Oregon climate.

I avoid plants with big shiny leaves because their glossiness will catch the eye and compete too much with flowering plants. English laurel (*Prunus laurocerasus*) and photinias (*Photinia* spp.) not only suffer from this fault but also grow too quickly and require endless clipping. I recommend slower-growing plants that top out at the desired height and need only a little clipping.

Broad-leaved evergreen shrubs also provide screening without requiring frequent trimming. They also need less maintenance but occupy more space. Laurustinus (*Viburnum tinus*), with its medium-size leaves and white fall and winter flowers followed by blue berries, has year-round interest. Japanese holly (*Ilex crenata*) offers small, rounded green leaves, while English holly (*Ilex aquifolium*) has the distinction of larger spiny leaves, and berries on some varieties. I am partial to the variegated English hollies, especially silver-margined holly (*I. aquifolium* 'Argentea Mariginata'), which is actually green edged with cream.

I like red clusterberry (*Cotoneaster lacteus*) for its graceful, arching shape and its cheerful bunches of red berries in late fall and winter. Strawberry tree (*Arbutus unedo*), a large shrub, intrigues me with its reddish brown bark and fall fruit that dangles like a cherry but has a strawberry's bumpy texture. In shade, taller *Rhododendron* and *Camellia* species and *Pieris japonica* make fine screening shrubs, with the added attraction of showy spring flowers.

Fences and masonry walls are more expensive than plants but have two strong advantages— immediate privacy and lower maintenance.

"Walls made of wood, stone or brick add solidity to the garden."

A Japanese-style fence and gate give the garden a theme.

Walls create a sense of enclosure.

A pond serves as a focal point, creating a soothing setting as soon as you enter this private space.

Creeping plants can be grown in cracks and crevices to soften the stone flooring.

Walls made of wood, stone or brick add solidity to the garden and offer interesting contrast with the softer texture of the plants. The posts, rails, caps and latticework of wooden fences contribute rhythmic patterns to the garden. Stone and brick add their own unique colors and textures along with a feeling of age and permanence. All of these constructed walls are invitations to train climbing roses, honeysuckle, clematis and other vines. Because they offer some protection from wind and cold, walls create shelter for growing marginally hardy plants.

CEILINGS FOR COZINESS

Although a garden room doesn't need a ceiling since the enclosed entry is close to the house, a canopy of some sort will help make a gradual transition from a looming building to the walls and plants of the garden. A tree canopy

is a good choice for that purpose, and it will provide some shade at the same time. When I plan a garden, I make sure to place trees far enough from the house—at least half the distance of the canopy's ultimate spread—to allow their branches to grow freely.

Structures can also provide a ceiling for the entry garden, preferably in a style that resembles the architecture of the home. A pergola can extend from the house and serve as a covered walkway. With trelliswork at the top, it can also support climbing plants and provide shade. A freestanding arbor toward the center of the entry garden can shade a seating area and be a focus of visual interest from inside the house. The same arbor placed closer to the front gate can function as a welcoming station for guests. I encourage my clients to construct built-in benches beneath arbors. The combined features of overhead flowering plants and shade

With a well-placed bench, the garden becomes an outdoor room. A bench allows admirers to sit and enjoy this garden rather than just pass by it on the way to the front door. A water garden makes for a tranquil view.

below make an irresistible place to sit and relax. Of course, if the entry is small and sunny space is limited, I sometimes forgo any shade-producing canopy and let the sky be the ceiling.

FLOORS FOR STABILITY

The garden floor should be a strong, silent partner—there to keep your feet dry, your furniture steady and your plants looking beautiful. One of the loveliest gardens I've ever visited has a floor made of brick pavers. Brick curbs edge the beds to retain soil and set off paths. The pink-orange tones of brick add a rich color that contrasts with and complements plants. I like a brick garden floor when the house is also made of brick; it unifies home and garden.

> *"I sometimes forgo any shade-producing canopy and let the sky be the ceiling."*

Poured concrete is another permanent material that affords a firm, dry surface. Because plain concrete forms a glaring white surface, I prefer exposed aggregate or tinted concrete to tone it down. A muted-color concrete allows your flowers to shine, not your floor.

Stone makes a handsome entry surface, adding age and character to the garden. The surface of some stone floors is irregular, creating interest but making it less predictable underfoot. However, the color and texture of stone are hard to beat. I love planting fragrant plants, such as flowering thymes (*Thymus* spp.), pinks (*Dianthus* spp.) and Corsican mint (*Mentha requienii*), in the crevices of stone floors. Treading on thyme and mint releases their scent, adding another dimension to the garden.

A less permanent material, such as crushed rock or fine gravel, can also surface the garden floor. Choose small (¼ in. or smaller) stones that will pack down firmly—larger gravel tends to slide underfoot. A curb or retaining edge can keep rock from creeping into the beds. Gravel and crushed rock need renewing from time to time, so they require more maintenance than poured concrete, stone or brick pavers. Another drawback is that weed seeds tend to germinate in floors made of crushed rock, but seedlings are easy enough to pull out. Actually, I think it's fun to leave occasional interesting self-sowers in the ground, à la John Brookes, the English garden designer who decorated his charming gravel paths with bold, gray-leaved mulleins (*Verbascum bombyciferum*).

No matter which style you select for your entry garden, there are endless possibilities for creating walls, ceilings and floors. Use these design principles as a starting point. The entry to your home belongs to you, and it should be yours to enjoy in comfort and privacy.

RUTH PARNALL

runs a general-practice design firm that emphasizes native plants and naturalistic design. She has written numerous articles and presented workshops on ecology for designers.

A Forest

in the

Front Yard

Fall colors blaze in a front yard filled with woodland plants. The ruddy autumn foliage of flowering dogwoods creates a rich backdrop for the fall golds of quaking aspen, sweet birch, and witch hazel. Hay-scented ferns along the sidewalks echo the seasonal theme.

WITH A CANOPY of sweet birch and quaking aspen overhead, and ferns and foamflower underfoot, you might think you're deep in the woods. Instead, you're standing in a small front yard in the middle of town. Or rather, a front yard transformed by a woodland-inspired redesign. Not long ago, this 3,300-square-foot, Northampton, Massachusetts, yard was unchanged by the seasons, a predictable cookie-cutter combination of foundation plants, lawn, and street trees—just like every other yard on the street. Now it's a parade of seasonal wonders. The annual march of time begins with the blossoms of wildflowers in spring, steps lively into the tree-dappled light of summer sun, pauses for the painterly colors of fall foliage, and finally surrenders to the stark shadows of leafless trees inked in the winter snow.

(ABOVE) Trees and tall ferns create a subtle fence. A sidewalk-side planting of black snakeroot, shield ferns, ostrich ferns, serviceberry, and viburnum serves as an informal barrier and provides a measure of privacy.

(RIGHT) Maturing trees intermingle with shrubs and herbaceous plants to create a garden that resembles the edge of a native forest.

The front-yard makeover began when the owners, Brinkley Thorne and Mazie Cox, were wrapping up the renovation of their late-Victorian house. They were ready to turn their attention to its front yard when they came to me for advice about garden design, which is my specialty. At first, Brink and Mazie wanted an English-style perennial garden enclosed by a white-picket fence that would protect the plants from kids, dogs, and basketballs. I con-

vinced them that a fence would only emphasize the smallness of the yard. I took them to other gardens, talked about the advantages of plantings with year-round appeal, and pointed out that a woodland garden would link the front of the house to a forested area in the back. Soon, Brink and Mazie were ready to try something different.

RE-CREATING A FOREST EDGE

Here in New England, fledgling forests advancing across former fields and farmlands are a common sight. The young trees, airy shrubs, and panoply of herbaceous plants that characterize the leading edge of a woodland restaking its claim on the landscape can also be a source of inspiration. And, as a landscape architect mindful of the need for reforestation, I find the theme useful for gardens large or small.

I was certain it would work for Brink and Mazie. The trees and tall ferns would create a subtle fence to keep kids from running pell-mell through the yard; an informal array of forest-floor plants wouldn't suffer much if a few were crushed by a runaway basketball; and the yard would just look bigger with its edges included in a woodland planting scheme. They agreed.

My plan for a garden with the character of a young forest edge included mostly regional natives, but the concept could have included plants of any origin, as long as they were visually in keeping with the woodland ecology. I wanted flowering herbaceous plants with small, loosely clustered flowers in subtle colors, and woody plants with a spindly, leggy habit. The leaves would be deep green, light green, or variegated. Any plant with those characteristics could work, as long as it wasn't of obvious alpine, desert, or seaside origin.

An In-Town Woodland Garden

Even a small city yard can seem like a woodland oasis. Capture the feel of the forest with a rich assortment of forest-floor plants shaded by native shrubs and small trees. Existing shade trees provide a high, leafy canopy that completes the effect.

Most of the trees I chose, such as serviceberry (*Amelanchier canadensis*) and sassafras (*Sassafras albidum*), have the typical character of their native habitat, the woodland edge. They have an airy growth, reach 15 to 20 ft. high, and are thin-trunked with small leaves. An existing pruned dogwood (*Cornus florida*) was thinned to look more like a shade-grown woodland native. I planted quaking aspen (*Populus tremuloides*) near it, and they slowly grew up through the dogwood's branches, just as they would in the wild.

Smaller niches were planted with shrubs that were open branched with small foliage, like those growing in the woods. So the garden would more closely resemble the nearby New England forest, I planted Northeastern natives such as pinxterbloom azalea (*Rhododendron*

Eastern Native Plants for a Woodland Garden

These plants are among the author's favorite hardy woodland plants. In addition to the attributes listed below, all of the plants mentioned here have colorful fall foliage, ranging from clear yellow to deep red.

SMALL TREES

SUN

Quaking aspen (*Populus tremuloides*)	Smooth, greenish-white bark.
Sassafras (*Sassafras albidum*)	Yellow flowers on candelabra-shaped branches, mitten-shaped leaves.

PART SHADE

Pagoda dogwood (*Cornus alternifolia*)	Spring-flowering edge tree, blue berries with red stems in fall.
Flowering dogwood (*C. florida*)	White flower bracts in spring, red fruits in fall.
Black haw (*Viburnum prunifolium*)	Deep purple fruit in fall.
Serviceberry (*Amelanchier canadensis*)	A cloud of small white blossoms in spring, followed by red berries in summer. Berries relished by birds.

SHADE TOLERANT

Common witch hazel (*Hamamelis virginiana*)	Smooth gray bark, arching trunks, yellow flowers in fall.

SHRUBS

PART SHADE

Pinxterbloom azalea (*Rhododendron periclymenoides*)	Delicate, fragrant, pink flowers in late spring.
Dwarf fothergilla (*Fothergilla gardenii*)	Brushy, white flowers in spring, red and yellow foliage in fall.
Bottlebrush buckeye (*Aesculus parviflora*)	Brushy, white flowers in early summer.
Mountain pieris (*Pieris floribunda*)	Clusters of white flowers in late spring.

WOODLAND FLOOR PLANTS

PART SHADE TO FULL SHADE

Hay-scented fern (*Dennstaedtia punctilobula*)	Sun-loving, dense foliage, fine fronds turn golden bronze after frost.

SUN TO PART SHADE

Christmas fern (*Polystichum acrostichoides*)	Cool green foliage.
Shield or wood ferns (*Dryopteris* spp.)	Lacy, 1 to 2 ft. tall, semi-evergreen.
Ostrich fern (*Matteuccia struthiopteris*)	4 ft. tall, bold outline.
White heath aster (*Aster ericoides*)	Profuse, white, starry flowers well into fall.
Wavy-leaved aster (*A. undulatus*)	Small lavender flowers.
Wild ginger (*Asarum canadense*)	Luminous, velvety-leaved ground cover.
Mayapple (*Podophyllum peltatum*)	Low shrublike mass, single white flower in spring.
Bloodroot (*Sanguinaria canadensis*)	Good ground cover through fall, very early single white flower.
Virginia creeper (*Parthenocissus quinquefolia*)	Ground cover (also climbs, but can be cut back if it climbs shrubs), deep red fall foliage.
Red baneberry (*Actaea rubra*)	Summer red berries on slender stalks.
Crested iris (*Iris cristata*)	Blue flowers in spring.
Foam flower (*Tiarella cordifolia*)	Ground cover with 8-in. spikes of tiny, white flowers in spring.
Black snakeroot (*Cimicifuga racemosa*)	White flowers grow on 6-ft.-tall spikes in early summer.
Wintergreen (*Gaultheria procumbens*)	Shiny, deep green leaves, tiny white flowers, brilliant red berries.

periclymenoides). For variety, I also added bottlebrush buckeye (*Aesculus parviflora*) and mountain pieris (*Pieris floribunda*), originally from the Southeast.

In this newly created woodland, the light changes with the seasons, so I selected a range of flowering plants to take advantage of every nuance. In sun-splashed spring, before the trees leaf out, bloodroot (*Sanguinaria canadensis*) and foamflower (*Tiarella cordifolia*) burst into bloom along with the dogwood and azalea. In shady summer, soothing green foliage takes over, but I also added a few flowering asters (*Aster* spp.) to the planting's sunnier edges. Once the leaves have fallen, the yellow blooms of witch hazel (*Hamamelis virginiana*) come into their own.

MANAGING A PLACE OF CHANGE

The owners of such a woodland garden need to cultivate certain virtues. They first have to be patient; it takes time for trees, shrubs, and herbaceous plants to grow large enough to intermingle as they do in the wild. Second, they must develop an appreciation of plants that goes beyond the fleeting beauty of flowers. And finally, they need to take pleasure in an ever-changing scene because a garden of woodland plantings is always evolving.

To establish and then maintain a garden with the quality of a young forest edge, we had to develop a long-term management program to meet its changing needs. At first, new trees and shrubs were too small to make much shade for ground-level plants, so we planted adaptable, shallow-rooted plants such as mayapple (*Podophyllum peltatum*) and crested

iris (*Iris cristata*). The small trees didn't produce enough leaves to form a moisture-conserving mulch of their own, so for a few years, Brink and Mazie had to collect extra leaves and spread them around the woodland garden each fall.

The leafy canopy gradually thickened, and the trees produced plenty of leaves for mulch. The increased shade also allowed us to add shade-tolerant plants like wild ginger (*Asarum canadense*) and partridgeberry (*Mitchella repens*). We anticipate that some cloning plants, such as the quaking aspen, will need to be cut back to the ground whenever they grow large enough to outscale the garden.

NATURE ENTERS THE NEIGHBORHOOD

Everyone who sees this garden learns something about a woodland plant community. Some have noticed that trees, shrubs, and herbaceous plants look at home in any front yard, especially when set against existing shade trees and broad-leaved evergreens. The garden inspired a few neighbors to expand their front-yard plantings all the way to the street, and some of the other lawns are slowly giving way to stone walks and clusters of woodland plants.

The woodland garden succeeded in changing an unpromising patchwork site into a beautiful setting that invites closer inspection. Its trees and shrubs are rich in flowers, fragrance, berries, and fall color. The whole front yard now reflects the changes of nature's unending cycles. For me, that is the best part of the garden.

"The leafy canopy gradually thickened, and the trees produced plenty of leaves for mulch."

CLINTON J. BEARDSLEY'S

firm, Metroscape, spe-
cializes in the design and
installation of gardens
for residential clients.
Many of his gardens have
been included on the
German Village House
and Garden annual tour.

An Engaging Entry Garden

A meandering stream-
side garden, complete
with stepping stones,
lures visitors from the
street to the front
door. (Photo taken at
A on site plan.)

IN A BIG GARDEN, individual plants and details
can be overlooked. But in a small garden every plant
and hardscaping detail is noticed and so must be
thought out by the designer.

I own a residential landscape design firm in
Columbus, Ohio. In 1990, I took on a challenging project—
designing a small entry garden that would integrate a
contemporary home into a 19th-century neighborhood.
The design and plant choices I made for this little garden
can be adapted to any garden with a similar site and
growing conditions.

FROM ALLEYWAY TO ENTRYWAY

My clients, Tom and Lenita Pepper, had lived in Japan,
where they acquired an appreciation for the simple beauty
of small Oriental gardens. They envisioned something similar for their entryway—a lush, secluded, informally planted garden with the sound of running water. My first chal-

Color and texture brighten a bland fence: Burgundy-leaved Japanese maple, long-needled Scotch pine and glossy-leaved blue holly spell textural relief for a plain fence. (Photo taken at C on site plan.)

lenge was to make the narrow passageway (a long, barren alley) seem more open. I also wanted to link the house to the neighborhood by creating an enticing view into the garden from the street, while still maintaining a secluded feeling. I set out to change this "bowling alley," as I called it, into a garden with the quiet beauty of those that the Peppers admired. The 8½- by 40-ft. space is enclosed on the long south side by a house with a block foundation and wood siding, and on the north

side by a 6-ft.-high wooden fence. So I had to choose plants that would grow with only the meager hour or two of direct sunlight that the site receives.

To meet the challenge, I joined the street and front door with a stream and a path. I surrounded these garden elements with closely clustered but mostly low plantings with a wide assortment of foliage colors and shapes, punctuated by shade-loving flowers. Glass doors at the street end offer the Peppers a

Streambed Cross Section

The site plan at right shows the layout of stream, stepping stones and plantings in the Pepper garden. The two drawings below show materials and methods used to make the streambed and pond.

To build a stream that would run downhill toward the house and pond, I raised the grade near the street entrance. I began by digging the streambed to a depth of about 6 in., deepening the stream as I went, and finally excavating the pond to about 2 ft. at its deepest point. I put 1 in. of sand over the entire watercourse and covered the sand with a liner of long-lasting rubber anchored along the stream

banks with heavy rocks. Covering the liner with river gravel made it look like a natural streambed. The water slowly wends its way from the spring through the garden to the pond and back, filling the garden with soothing sound.

After the stream was in place, I constructed the path: a combination of large and small stepping-stones that border the stream in some places and cross it in others. I excavated to a depth of about 8 in., put down a 4-in. base of crushed stone and stone dust, and tamped it into place. Then I topped the base with sand and laid flagstones.

SITE PLAN

POND DETAIL

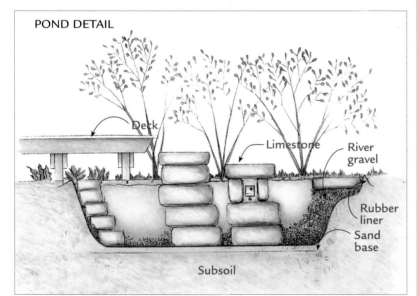

STREAMBED CROSS SECTION

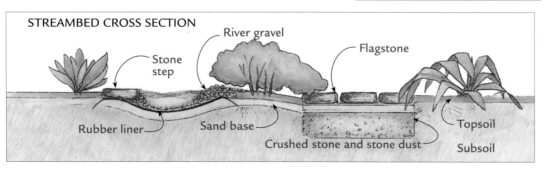

Glass doors (rather than a solid gate) were placed at the street end, offering a glimpse of the garden beyond.

Gentle curves encourage visitors to slow down, making the space feel larger than it is.

A weeping beech, white-spotted pulmonaria, and Japanese blood grass accent the streamside planting with color.

A meandering streambed draws visitors from the street to the front door.

(Photo taken at B on site plan.)

glimpse into the garden from outside and a more expansive view from within.

The stream that runs the length of the garden starts at the street as a spring—a small, lined pond with water fed through a recirculating pump—at the base of a weeping beech tree (*Fagus sylvatica* 'Pendula') and empties into a pond at the front door. I placed gravel along some of the banks, creating mini beaches.

To make the garden look as large as possible, I made a deck at the front door from an industrial aluminum grate, the kind used for catwalks in factories. Next, I extended the pond beneath this see-through grating and planted ground covers at the pond's edge. Then I set large stones into the pond to form a bridge across the water and steps leading up to the deck.

DESIGN WITH PLANTS

I carefully chose and placed vertical-growing plants to divert attention from the length of the garden. The key elements here are the beech tree, which frames the garden view from the street, and, at the opposite end, a serviceberry (*Amelanchier canadensis*), which forms a canopy over the front door. Midway against the plain fence, I planted a Japanese maple (*Acer palmatum* var. *dissectum*), whose finely cut, reddish-tinged leaves add grace and color. Next to the maple, the long needles of a Scotch pine (*Pinus sylvestris*) cover the fence all year. I hid the house's foundation with blue hollies (*Ilex × meserveae* 'Blue Princess'), yews (*Taxus × media* 'Hicksii') and blood-twig dogwoods (*Cornus sanguinea*).

For maximum impact, I chose ground covers that had interesting flowers and foliage, namely, sweet woodruff (*Galium odoratum*) for its small white flowers in spring and its

glossy, whorled leaves. I also added lemon thyme (*Thymus serpyllum*), which offers tiny purple flowers in spring and imparts a lemon scent to the air when its mat of delicate leaves is stepped on. Allegheny foamflower (*Tiarella wherryi*) provides clouds of white flowers in early summer, and its feathery, knee-high foliage combines well with the fronds of Christmas ferns (*Polystichum acrostichoides*), Japanese painted ferns (*Athyrium niponicum* 'Pictum') and red-tipped Japanese blood grass (*Imperata cylindrica* 'Rubra').

The result of my efforts is a garden that provides the Peppers with a peaceful oasis in an urban environment—a place where they and their guests can stop and reflect.

A deck made from aluminum grating allows visitors a birds-eye view of the pond. Stepping-stones link the garden to the deck. (Photo taken at D on site plan.)

> *"For maximum impact, I chose ground covers that had interesting flowers and foliage."*

ALAN EARP

is a former classics pro-
fessor and retired presi-
dent of Brock University
in St. Catharines,
Ontario. He now spends
most of his time tending
his gardens in Niagara-
on-the-Lake.

Designing a
Lawnless
Front Yard

Form and foliage carry
the day. Trees, shrubs,
and ground covers—
both evergreen and
deciduous—provide
plenty of variety and
interest in all four
seasons.

A PPREHENSION GREW in our conserva-
tive neighborhood the day the crane
arrived. Those who saw it dangling 48-ft.
posts above our building lot could be for-
given for thinking that another monster
house was under way. Such fears, however, were soon
allayed. The retirement house we built, if unconventional
in structure, is actually quite small and blends well with its
surroundings. But curiosity was again aroused when neighbors, stopping by to chat as I began planting the front yard,
learned that there would not be any lawn.

Foregoing a lawn was not a rash decision, or a political or
environmental statement. Nor did we have any illusions
about lower maintenance. Rather it was a practical
response to space constraints. Our previous garden had
been 75 ft. by 200 ft.; this new space is just 25 ft. by 75 ft.
Omitting a lawn simply allowed for much more room to
garden.

A winding path connects house and driveway. The author used salvaged stone to pave a winding path through his front yard, breaking it up into smaller spaces.

Occupying the house at Christmas, Jeanette and I spent the rest of the winter planning. Our goal for the front yard was to create an orderly yet natural-looking garden that would be of interest both from the street and from the house, and over all four seasons, including the long Canadian winter. In order to accomplish this, we relied on form, texture, and long-lasting foliage, with flowers playing a supporting role. We also varied the height of our plantings to create greater topographic interest, and chose plants that complemented the faintly Asian character of our brick and cedar house.

PATHS LEAD THE WAY

Spring came, and even the cat was leaving muddy footprints everywhere, so our first priority was to put in a solid path from our front door to the road. Fortunately, there were enough bricks left over from construction of the house for a path. But we still needed another, longer path to connect our new brick path with the gravel driveway at the side. As luck would have it, a neighbor was breaking up his patio, and he had no use for the stones. Their random shape allowed for a more sinuous, curving path, which pleased us, providing, as it does, a contrast to the long, straight facade of the house. In addition to reducing muddy footprints, these paths also serve to break the garden into smaller areas, which proved helpful as we were deciding on plant groupings.

A LOW HEDGE OF BOXWOOD DEFINES THE GARDEN

We wanted to define the garden area and to give the empty yard some living structure, so we planted a hedge of boxwood (*Buxus sempervirens*). At the same time, we wanted the eye to be able to move beyond the hedge, so we kept it low—only about 15 in. tall. To prevent it from becoming boring, we punctuated the

Swaths of cotoneaster subdivide the yard. This meandering shrub row crosses both paths, linking the yard from end to end while creating separate little garden areas.

(INSET) There's no shortage of color in the author's garden, even though it relies primarily on foliage and structure to engage.

hedge with little clusters of taller specimens of box in various shapes and we interrupted the longest stretch with an opening at its midpoint.

I used a few extra stones from my neighbor's patio to form the beginnings of a connecting path toward this opening. This path, however, disappears almost immediately, enveloped in a sea of low-growing *Veronica whitleyi*, with its wavy, gray-blue foliage. Faux paths like this one help create a sense of something beyond, adding a touch of mystery, which is difficult to achieve in such a small space.

"With the major lines of the garden established, the project began to feel a bit more manageable."

Faux paths help make a small space feel larger. The author created a number of paths in his yard, like this one of moss-engulfed stones, that simply trail off. They add structure and lend an air of mystery.

A SHRUBBY BACKBONE LINKS THE GARDEN FROM END TO END

Thus far, the stone path was the only fluid line in the garden. We wanted more curves—as well as varied plant heights—to offset the rigidity and uniformity of house and hedge. We started with a swath of rockspray cotoneaster (*Cotoneaster horizontalis*) weaving its way through the garden lengthwise, crossing both paths and giving the yard its backbone. We reinforced the rockspray cotoneaster with a band of low-growing *C. dammeri* beside it. These shrubs, in addition to providing flowers in the spring, berries in the winter, and leaves of contrasting textures throughout the year, also serve to link the different parts of the garden, making them all feel a part of the whole.

With the major lines of the garden established, the project began to feel a bit more manageable. We began to fill in, both reinforcing the existing lines in the garden, and adding new ones. For example, we used moss and stepping stones in places to create a sense of passage—sometimes real and sometimes illusory.

At the northern edge of the property, a problem became an opportunity. Despite a great deal of shoveling, I still had not gotten the level right here nor worked out how to finish off this end of the garden. We had a pile of clean river stone left over from the construction of the house, however, and it soon suggested a Japanese-inspired stone river, which could serve both as an occasional path and as a storm drain.

TREES AND SHRUBS GIVE A VERTICAL DIMENSION

There were still problem areas. One, a windowless expanse of brick (our garage wall), called both for height and some illusion of depth. We put in a single beech tree (*Fagus sylvatica*), which covered up a good portion of the garage wall and resonated with the small grove of beech beyond the driveway. We still needed to create some depth here, but we did not have much space in which to work. We settled on seven euonymus (*Euonymus fortunei* 'Sarcoxie') standards of varying height. These will eventually grow together, a mass of mopheads on matchsticks, providing a dense, eye-level circle of broad-leaved evergreens against the brick.

At one corner of the house a window runs from sill to roof. Beside it we planted a paperbark maple (*Acer griseum*). In winter, its peeling bark provides visual interest, and in the summer, the foliage is sparse enough not to block the view. A mounding Japanese maple (*Acer palmatum* var. *dissectum*) at its foot contrasts in form and foliage. Another Japanese maple ('Oshio beni') partially screens the kitchen window from the street. It also serves as a leafy staging area for birds, providing entertainment for anyone at the kitchen sink.

FLOWERS, TOO, HAVE A PLACE

Even in a garden that relies primarily on texture, form, and foliage for interest, flowers have a role. We wanted patches or accents of color flowering successively over as long a season as possible. In addition to the early-flowering bulbs, we used Siberian irises for their exquisite, though short-lived, flowers and daylilies for their wide color range and long season. We planted clematis, too, in a few places, training them onto slender trellises in some cases and just letting them sprawl loosely through the shrubs elsewhere.

In spring, ground covers provide their own expanses of color. A number of species of *Veronica*, in particular, come into their own. In May, *V. whitleyi* forms a sea of blue beyond the boxwood harbor while pools of white *V. repens* provide color within. By July, a band of darker-green *V. allionii*—on both sides of the boxwood—is studded with small, blue spires.

GRASSES HOLD SWAY, SOME EVEN IN WINTER

We didn't want a lawn, but that didn't mean there wasn't a place for grasses in our garden. In a couple of spots we grouped a large blue oatgrass (*Helictotrichon sempervirens*) with half a dozen or so small blue fescues (*Festuca glauca*), having fun with its suggestion of a mother and her brood. We also grouped colorful and durable sweet flag (*Acorus gramineus* 'Variegatus') with contrasting leatherleaf sedge (*Carex buchananii*) and the welcome winter bronze of *C. comans*. Two tiny clumps of mosquito grass (*Bouteloua gracilis*) are quite engaging over several months, when their seed pods appear to be hovering over them.

The effect of the taller of these grasses is most pronounced when they stand out against

the winter snow. The shorter ones are buried by it, as is the dense mat of *C. dammeri*. Berries and all, though, the long, skeletal backbone of the rockspray cotoneaster rises above the snow, winding its way through the white expanse to join the boxwood, starkly defining boundaries that the perennials will blur again in spring.

A stone river defines one end of the garden. It also functions as a storm drain and occasional path.

"Even in a garden that relies primarily on texture, form, and foliage for interest, flowers have a role."

GALLERY OF IDEAS

4

BACKYARDS ARE WHERE GARDENERS most often engage in their freedom of expression. Some prefer to keep it simple, providing access to the natural, woodland garden. Others go all out, reshaping the terrain from flat to rolling or from rolling to flat.

In this section, you'll discover a variety of innovative ideas for transforming your property. Most of these examples are from backyards, but many of their concepts can be applied to any place on your property. In fact, the playground garden that you'll read about, which you would expect to find in a backyard, was actually created in this homeowner's front yard.

As one landscape designer said earlier in this book, "The most important question to ask yourself is 'What if?'" So follow the lead of these designers, and do a little "what if" planning in your own yard.

KONRAD GAUDER

is a landscape designer and contractor. He and his wife, Denise Snaer-Gauder, a landscape architect, own Landsculpture, a Berkeley, California-based design-and-build firm.

From Flat
to Gently Rolling
Terrain

Berms and a dry streambed transform a flat, boxy backyard. Here, a large stone slab bridges the dry streambed, and a stepping-stone path circles the backyard.

W HEN MY SISTER and her husband asked our landscaping firm to design and build the garden for their new home in Vancouver, Washington, we were both flattered and challenged. The budget was more than adequate, but the property offered little aesthetic promise. Their 45- by 85-ft. backyard, which consisted of little more than lawn, was boxy, flat, and somewhat sunken.

To combat the monotony of the small, rectangular lawn, we suggested changing the terrain from flat to rolling by creating a series of berms. While the rolling berms would add height, we also wanted to create depth, so we designed a naturalistic dry streambed. The streambed was laid out diagonally, bisecting the lot, creating near and far spaces separated by the stream. This also helped eliminate the boxy feeling of the property, as diagonal lines tend to lead the eye toward more distant spaces and borrowed views to make the garden feel larger.

A DRY STREAMBED ADDS DEPTH

When building a dry streambed, you want to create the illusion of a passage of water. Gentle curves in the streambed add authenticity and create a sense of rhythm. Boulders placed strategically in and around the streambed add credibility and help to frame the composition, while rounded river stones fill the streambed, adding dimension and breaking up the terrain. Plantings add a nice finishing touch.

Dry streambeds should be located on low ground, with the surrounding earth graded higher to imply running water's erosive tendencies. And while a dry streambed remains dry most of the time, it also serves an important role handling runoff during rainstorms. So when grading a site, not only does your streambed have to be lower than the surrounding terrain, but it also must follow a downward grade so that water runs through it without puddling. In this case, the streambed runs to a hidden storm drain, where the runoff is carried away.

We used two kinds of rock in this garden. For the larger boulders, we opted for locally quarried basalt. Some of these boulders were used in and along the edge of the streambed to imply continuous geologic ridges over which the stream meandered. In the streambed itself, we used rounded river cobbles of various sizes. The larger cobbles were rescued from a highway construction site. These stones made the streambed a success by adding a realistic scale to the design.

A mix of plants and boulders helped create a natural-looking beginning and end to the streambed. At the stream's "origin," we installed a bubbling boulder, which had been drilled so that water could be plumbed through it. The boulder sits on a metal screen over a concrete basin, and the pump is located in the basin. This feature, though not essential, adds the sight and sound of water year-round, even though the water does not flow the length of the streambed.

Ornamental grasses like *Acorus gramineus* 'Ogon', *A. g.* 'Variegatus', leather leaf sedge (*Carex buchananii*), sweet flag (*Acorus calamus*), blue oat grass (*Helictotrichon sempervirens*), and soft rush (*Juncus effusus*), along with irises (*Iris* spp.) and bog plants, punctuate the stream bank, much as they might in nature. They add authenticity to the setting when grouped in and around the stream and when juxtaposed with the boulders.

BERMS GIVE THE FEELING OF ROLLING TERRAIN

The term "berm" is used to describe a mounded, sometimes undulating, and usually longitudinal earth form. The berms we created in this garden flank the streambed on both sides, and are shaped to conform to the meandering streambed. As such, their shapes are softly curved. The largest, which is located in the far corner of the property, measures roughly 30 ft. by 40 ft. and rises 4 ft. from the original grade. Opposite that, on the other side of the streambed, another berm planted primarily in turf grass measures 18 ft. by 35 ft. and is about 2 ft. high.

In addition to using excavated soil from the dry streambed, we brought in about 40 cubic yards of loamy soil to create our mounds. All of the soil, along with the rocks for the streambed, was moved by hand or with the help of a motor-propelled flatbed carrier.

To create a destination in the garden, a small, stone terrace was placed at the top of the largest berm at the rear of the property. From this point, a meandering stepping stone path leads back toward the deck, crossing the stream with a large stone slab. It then circles the garden, leading back to the stone terrace.

Although one berm is mostly lawn, the other features plantings for year-round interest in color, texture, and form. So they would blend in naturally with the woodland beyond—a northwestern rainforest—mostly native plants were used. They were sited in microclimates, such as the moist streamside and cool woodland edge, similar to their natural habitats. Thimbleberry (*Rubus odoratus*), dogwoods (*Cornus* spp.), alders (*Alnus* spp.), and a variety of ferns—such as maidenhair fern (*Adiantum pedatum*), deer fern (*Blechnum spicant*), coastal wood fern (*Dryopteris arguta*), lady fern (*Athyrium felix-femina*), and western sword fern (*Polysticum munitum*)—were planted along the woodland edge. Evergreen huckleberry (*Vaccinium ovatum*), salal (*Gautheria shallon*), and common bearberry (*Arctostaphylos uva-ursi*) made a natural transition from streambed to lawn areas. And finally, the planting beds were mulched to inhibit weed growth, conserve moisture, and prevent erosion.

This small backyard was just a flat, rectangular lawn. Now it has rolling berms, a curving dry streambed, a deck for entertaining, and attractive plantings.

A DECK ADDS FURTHER DIMENSION

Just outside the kitchen door, next to the family room, we constructed a deck over a smaller, existing concrete patio. It was designed primarily for entertaining, so we built in benches that double as railings. Both the deck and benches were stained gray to match the house, as well as to protect the wood.

The deck serves as a viewing platform in the sense that it belongs more to the house than to the garden. It conveys an air of light-

Five Years from Start to Finish

From excavated yard to flourishing garden in just a few years. This series of photos shows the garden during excavation (1994), not long after planting (1995), and after the garden has had time to grow (1999). All photos were taken from approximately the same location.

ness as it partially projects over the streambed. Although it is elevated, it is not the highest point in the garden. Indeed, one can look down on the deck from the seating area atop the highest berm.

Because the deck serves as a spring point into the garden, we placed a number of plants alongside it. On the south end is a lovely tri-color beech (*Fagus sylvatica* 'Purpurea tricolor'); a pair of paperbark maples (*Acer griseum*) anchor the north end. Both the beech and maple offer a leafy canopy, and their exfoliating bark, which can be inspected up close, creates visual interest in every season. Oregon grape holly (*Mahonia aquifolium*) and leather leaf sedge are planted nearby, their fronds and leaves softening the deck's hard edges.

The garden has provided many hours of pleasure for my sister and her family. Unlike the original landscape, which offered little interest, the yard now draws you in, allowing you to feel like there are many routes from which to choose, as well as fantasies to pursue.

"Although one berm is mostly lawn, the other features plantings for year-round interest in color, texture, and form."

From Wooded Lot *to Woodland* Path

DAVID J. CALHOON

is a member of the Green Bay Botanical Garden and Door County Land Trust, as well as Ridges Sanctuary in Bailey's Harbor, Wisconsin.

Let woodland paths meander, revealing a new surprise around each bend. Curved paths also encourage you to slow down and enjoy the scenery.

AS A BOY, I SPENT hours in the woods. My parents owned a cottage on Senator Lake near Crivitz, Wisconsin, in the midst of the Nicolet National Forest, where we went every weekend and for vacations. I remember walking through the woods with my father, who taught me the names of trees and explained the lay of the land, which was somewhat swampy and had natural drainage to the lake. He suggested I build a bridge over one of these areas, making it easier to access the woods. I accomplished this task and then started clearing some trails. My father and family would often check on my progress, enjoying the walks through the woods. I enjoyed the fact that everyone liked the trails.

As an adult, I am fortunate to own a wonderfully diverse piece of property bordering the southwestern shores of the bay of Green Bay. My woods, mostly eastern deciduous forest, have many distinct habitats for plants

155

and wildlife, and so, wanting to make the most of the property, I started bringing my trails to areas that interested me. The woods are filled with hidden treasures like jack-in-the-pulpit (*Arisaema triphyllum*), *trillium*, mosses, and lichens. And so by blending in a few of my favorite plants like *Ligularia* and ferns, I have created a very natural woodland garden.

QUIET TRAILS CAN UNITE YOU WITH NATURE

With the paths, I can share the woods with wildlife. The woodland edge supplies ideal browsing areas for the white-tailed deer that share my trails. Raccoons play by the stream, and woodpeckers eat the insects from decaying trees. I even use sand in some areas to provide dusting places for mourning doves and whippoorwills. Clover, which I plant with a

salt shaker, provides excellent ground cover, a wonderful scent, and good eating for rabbits and insects.

Another way I have added to this wildlife microhabitat is by building brush piles. This solves the problem of where to dispose of all the brush created from clearing the paths, and also provides shelter for small animals like cottontail rabbits, red foxes, and chipmunks, as well as low nesting birds. I use a crisscross technique of piling the brush to make pockets for nesting, and have built three brush piles that are out of sight on the edges of the property. It's also important to leave some branches and logs to decay in the woods, enriching the soil for future plant life.

WOODLAND PATHS SHOULD MEANDER

My curved pathways wind through the woods, revealing a new surprise around every corner. They follow the natural terrain of the land—following ridge lines, meandering up and down hills, and winding around trees. A little stream trickles through my woodland property. Many of my trails follow along its banks, so I can enjoy the wetland area with its turk's-cap lilies (*Lilium superbum*), mayapples (*Podophyllum peltatum*), and wild Geranium; in early spring, the marsh marigolds (*Caltha palustris*) are especially pretty. I've even built a couple of bridges to cross the stream, always making sure they are wide enough for my garden tractor to pass across easily.

While most of my trails are wide enough for two people to walk side by side, I sometimes like to narrow the path and wind through the shelter of full-grown trees like hickories, red oaks, and mature cottonwoods, which, because of their rough, weathered bark, are interesting to feel.

(ABOVE) Place benches along your woodland garden trail. Use scrap lumber or even an old log for places to sit for a spell.

(LEFT) Once the basic trail is broken, use a mower to maintain it. To keep his paths nicely groomed, the author mows them every two weeks in summer.

"The woods are filled with hidden treasures like jack-in-the-pulpit, trillium, mosses, and lichens."

When designing woodland paths, add points of interest like this old wagon wheel.

CREATE POINTS OF INTEREST ALONG THE WAY

Even though my paths meander, they also provide points of interest. For instance, the gateway to my garden trails is a rustic covered bridge built from 120-year-old lumber salvaged from a nearby barn.

"I'm very selective when removing large trees and shrubs because it takes a long time to replace them."

I like to concentrate on roomlike clearings, usually with a view or a focal point, that offer opportunities to pause for a short rest or quiet observation. For my favorite clearing, I chose the highest point of my property: a ridge from which I can see most of my land. It has some mature white pines that provide a nice floor of rich brown needles, a welcome change from grass and moss.

Some of the most intriguing features along my trails are the wildflower patches. I've added lots of plants, like ferns, mayapples, trilliums, and jack-in-the-pulpits. And I like to imitate the waves of color seen in nature. For instance, in the summer I see waves of wild blue chicory (*Cichorium intybus*) and miles of wild yellow daisies along roadsides, so I duplicate these colors in my wildflower meadows with black-eyed Susan (*Rudbeckia* spp.), bee balm (*Monarda didyma*), and daffodils. I also like to add objects of interest, such as natural-looking birdhouses and signs of rough wood that offer uplifting sayings. Trees with unique growth patterns and twisted trunks are always interesting, as are footbridges, especially when one shows up where you least expect it.

Because both country life and simpler times appeal to me, I also use wagon wheels, farming implements, and hand tools. Then I add structures like benches and arbors so I can stop and sit awhile; sometimes a stump cut at the right height is just as comfortable.

One of my favorite areas of the garden is a very quiet spot near the far end of my property. Here, the path branches off in three directions, a perfect place for a bench I use often. From this spot I can hear the running water of the stream and enjoy the songs of birds. It's a real temple for the soul, a place where I can be at peace with myself and nature.

CLEARING PATHS IS PHYSICAL

There's no getting around it. Clearing wooded areas for paths is a physical activity that requires a lot of work. When scouting out new areas for trails, I select the path of least resistance and work a little bit of it at a time. It has taken me 10 years to clear my woodland trails, and I'm still not totally finished. I do most of the work in the early spring, limbing up trees and adding plants as I go during their normal bloom so I can see how they look.

First, I clear the big stuff with a chain saw. I'm very selective when removing large trees and shrubs because it takes a long time to replace them. I find it best to have the trails meander around the mature trees. When I think a tree needs to be cut back, I use brush cutters (like an Army-surplus machete), loppers, and sometimes my hands to pull out the growth. As a precaution, I wear long pants, a long-sleeved shirt, and gloves to keep from getting scratched.

When I clear roomlike areas, I first cut the surrounding brush close to the ground with either a pair of loppers or a chain saw. I then use a telescoping saw to trim any overhanging limbs (up to about 7 ft.), leaving the rest to create a sheltered feel. Next, I rake the leaves, and then fill any holes or low spots and level them off so I don't trip.

Once I break the basic trail, I use a mower to take care of the small stuff. To keep the trails nicely groomed, I mow at least every two weeks and carry the loppers along the trails for touch-up work. In time, grasses and moss will take root. A little sulfur sifted from a strainer will encourage moss growth.

There are many challenges in clearing a woodland path. You'll face steep hills that need steps, and wet areas that need to be filled in with gravel or dealt with by laying logs across the top. Perhaps the most challenging feat of all is facing the density of the forest and just getting started. But with a little patience, lots of persistence, and some ingenuity, you'll soon have your own woodland trail to explore with friends.

Wildflowers make up some of the most interesting parts of a woodland trail, which is why the author has planted ferns, mayapples, trilliums, and jack-in-the-pulpits along his paths.

"I wanted to design an ecologically responsible garden that evokes a sense of timelessness, place, and peace."—Jeni Webber

"Since privacy was of the utmost importance, I developed a series of defined spaces, each with a strong sense of enclosure."—Gary Keim

"I designed this garden to create a place for the clients to indulge their developing fascination with water plants."—Scott Lankford

STEVE SILK

is a contributing editor for *Fine Gardening*. His garden was featured on The Garden Conservancy Tour.

Redesigning *the* Backyard

Three garden designers were challenged to transform a simple space into a backyard garden retreat. Their unique ideas resulted in three very different treatments of the same space.

THROW OPEN THE BACK DOOR, step outside, and survey your empire. What have you got? Let's say it's a boring sweep of turf with all the allure of an overgrown billiard table. Across that monotonous swath of green lies another monotonous swath of green—your neighbor's backyard. And just beyond that stands their house. You've got an unobstructed view of the place, which is exactly what you don't want. Backyards, after all, should be a place where your imagination can run wild, a place of sanctuary where you can entertain with style and relax in grace. And they should be places where gardeners can realize their wildest dreams.

We asked three designers to envision a backyard like that—one filled with potential, but not much else. And we gave them a few more particulars too: a space 50 by 100 ft., bounded on the south side by the house. The yard is flat and devoid of trees. It's sunny and the soil is good. The hypothetical clients are a couple in their 50s who work full-time but still enjoy gardening and hosting small dinner parties. The kids have left home, so the clients have time and some money—about $25,000—to devote to a backyard makeover that they hope will give them a little outdoor privacy. They're willing to do some of the work to cut costs and they look forward to tending the gardens they envision.

For each designer, we suggested a different approach to restyling the basic backyard. Jeni Webber, of Oakland, California, would create a rich flower garden—decorated with interesting trees, shrubs, and garden structures—highlighted by a hidden oasis. Gary Keim, of Swarthmore, Pennsylvania, was to design a naturalistic garden with a secluded feel. It is screened by unusual flowering trees and shrubs. It also features a garden structure and borders where the owners could putter with perennials. And we asked R. Scott Lankford, of Seattle, Washington, to create a private, pond-dotted retreat with a formal flair. For a look at the designers' plans, plant lists, and a sketch of the picture in their mind's eye, read on.

—Steve Silk

JENI WEBBER
Diagonal Design Emphasizes a Sense of Movement

I wanted to design an ecologically responsible garden that evokes a sense of timelessness, place, and peace. I intended for the clients to develop their garden in stages and let it establish gradually. They do want a "sense of a garden" to develop quickly though, especially to establish immediate privacy.

My design incorporates classic garden elements like allees and arbors in a non-traditional layout that emphasizes the sense of movement and passage.

To make the garden feel larger, I divided the space into three distinct areas: the patio, lawn, and perennial area near the house; the central garden with arbors and yew allees; and the secluded oasis at the far end. A wire fence surrounding the entire garden will be quickly covered with rampant, colorful, and fragrant vines—such as jasmine, evergreen clematis, and trumpet vines—to provide privacy within the first growing season. Larger, spreading trees along the periphery will create screening yet avoid casting too much shade on the inner beds. Walls, arbors, and columnar trees will give vertical structure to the garden, leaving large open areas for perennial plantings.

The area closest to the house will invite quick visits for coffee by the knot garden or breakfast beneath the grapevine-covered arbor. This arbor heightens the sense of enclosure and adds a feeling of depth to the knot garden, lawn, and surrounding perennial garden, where I envisioned a typical English-style border with

Plants for a Lush Flower Garden

PLANTS
NUMBERED WOODY PLANTS

1 *Malus* 'Fuji'

2 'Swan Hill' olive (*Olea europaea* 'Swan Hill')

3 'Los Altos' sequoia (*Sequoia sempervirens* 'Los Altos')

4 'Royal Purple' smoke bush (*Cotinus coggygria* 'Royal Purple')

5 'Cherokee' crepe myrtle (*Lagerstroemia indica* 'Cherokee')

6 Japanese maple (*Acer palmatum* 'Atropurpureum')

7 *Magnolia sprengeri* var. *diva*

PATIO AREA

The knot in the knot garden is composed of wall germander (*Teucrium chamaedrys*) and lavender cotton (*Santolina chamaecyparissus*), and ornamented with ground covers: snow in summer (*Cerastium tomentosum*), *Lobelia erinus*, and thyme (*Thymus pseudolanuginosus*).

The herb garden is bordered by boxwood (*Buxus* spp.) and contains a variety of culinary herbs and several rows of long-blooming 'Munstead' lavender (*Lavandula angustifolia* 'Munstead').

Surrounding the lawn is a colorful perennial garden, where plants with high water needs are concentrated. It is accented by flowering shrubs like princess flower (*Tibouchina urvilleana*), 'Royal Red' butterfly bush (*Buddleia davidii* 'Royal Red'), *Loropetalum chinense* 'Razzleberri', and *Hydrangea macrophylla* 'Forever Pink'.

CENTRAL GARDEN AREA

Near the allée are planting areas containing lots of drought-tolerant perennials with silver, blue-green, purple, and green foliage and pastel blooms. They include shrubs like lilac hibiscus (*Alyogyne huegelii*), weeping willowleaf pear (*Pyrus salicifolia* 'Pendula'), 'Rose Glow' barberry (*Berberis thunbergii* 'Rose Glow'), angels' trumpets (*Brugmansia* × *candida*), and *Buddleia davidii* var. *nanhoensis*.

THE OASIS

In the far back, by the oasis, a canopy of queen palm (*Syagrus romanzoffiana*) and a hedge of 'Los Altos' sequoia (*Sequoia sempervirens* 'Los Altos') preside over a planting of 'Rancho White' lily of the Nile (*Agapanthus* 'Rancho White'), 'Limelight' licorice plant (*Helichrysum petiolare* 'Limelight'), *Sedum album*, *Clematis* 'Henryi', *Wisteria floribunda* 'Longissima Alba', and jasmine (*Jasminum polyanthum*).

most plants in groups of three and occasional specimen plantings for accent. A saturated color theme with lime-green and purple foliage will create a dynamic medley in this area. A garden folly—a bathtub with working shower—is on a direct axis with the knot garden.

At cross axis to the lawn lies the central garden area, where yews line a curving path that leads to an allee which, again, is at cross axis. Plantings here are looser, with larger, interplanted drifts of pastel perennials, grasses, and shrubs. At one end of the allee sits a garden bench, while a water weir—a sort of small waterfall—terminates the axis in the far corner. Here, there's a choice of routes, either the allee or a small path through an informally planted back area anchored by a large olive tree. Soft foliage colors of blue and green contrast with the burgundy of smoke bush (*Cotinus coggygria* 'Royal Purple' or 'Velvet Cloak'), 'Chameleon' euphorbia (*Euphorbia dulcis* 'Chameleon'), and *Pennisetum setaceum* 'Rubrum'.

Down the allee and to the right is a lush oasis enclosed with hedges and tumbledown walls, like those of an old ruin, which will be covered with vines and small plants. In classic alignment with the entrance is the water weir which will flow over a seating wall into a semicircular pool. Flanking the pool along a low, enclosing wall will be four formed-concrete columns wrapped with wisteria, which will also cover the bent-copper arbor above. A dining table and benches created from sanded, old boards will add to the timeless feeling.

To save money, the clients will install as much as possible themselves, so I adapted the hardscape to basic construction abilities. For economic as well as ecological reasons, I used recycled materials whenever possible. From a salvage yard, I got copper for the arbors, an old door for the entrance to the walled garden, and a claw-foot bathtub (with shower) to use

as a water folly. Instead of stone, I used old, broken concrete pavement—available free from the city—for paving, arbors, and walls. Treating the concrete with iron sulfate gives it rich ochre hues with the patina of age.

I estimate costs to be about $2,500 for soil preparation, and $10,000 for the wood fencing, broken concrete walls and paving, gravel paths, pool, water weir, and the arbors. Plants and sod will run about $5,000, with the owners planting ground covers and perennials and doing the sod work. The bathtub water folly and garden shed will add another $3,000. To make the garden ecologically sound, I planned to conserve water by using a drip irrigation system laid so that parts of it can be turned off as plants mature and require less water. It should cost about $3,000 if installed by the owners.

My design is intended to create a sense of a mature garden quickly. The strength of the architecture—the ruin walls, arbors, trellises, and the sharply defined lawn and patio spaces—help to establish a strong sense of place immediately. The plant budget includes a few good-sized trees that will already look established, and a number of colorful shrubs that will look nice even when small. With the excellent soil base, the plants will fill in very nicely in two or three years. In the meantime, annuals could fill in the gaps.

GARY KEIM
Trees and Shrubs Provide Privacy and a Long Season of Interest

The design I created divides the lot into distinct sections, each of which serves a specific function. They are connected by axes linked directly to windows of the principal rooms on the south side of the house. Since privacy was of the utmost importance to these clients, I developed a series of defined spaces, each with a strong sense of enclosure. This treatment provides a series of intimate spaces and makes the garden feel larger. Visitors strolling through the garden will experience a sense of discovery as they move from area to area. Every space has a distinct feeling, whether it's a change in color scheme, a different paving material underfoot, or simply a new palette of plants. Each garden space has a mixture of fast-growing shrubs which will rapidly provide screening each spring. I envisioned using these multilayered spaces as a baffle for neighboring views.

The plan view shows the geometry of the garden areas, which make use of strong lines that accentuate the axes and give much form to the garden. After all, in a temperate climate where garden-related activities cease for nearly half the year, a strong outline of garden shapes provides interest and structure for those many months the garden is dormant.

Areas for entertaining are located near the house. One is a large stone terrace which both the kitchen and dining room open on to, so serving is easy. Around the terrace, summer-blooming shrubs form a screen of flowers and foliage which serves to hide views of neighboring houses. The flower gardens near the house are orchestrated to peak at the height of the

"Visitors strolling through the garden will experience a sense of discovery as they move from area to area."—Gary Keim

summer, when outdoor living is most popular. From here, a pergola shaded by vines provides a shadowy tunnel leading to the adjoining room and creates an axial view focusing on an elaborately planted container. The pergola also serves as an aerial screen to make the dining terrace more intimate.

Another distinct space is the privet-enclosed room. Deliberately void of flowering plants, except for the container, this space gives contrast by virtue of its spare simplicity, and provides a restful diversion from the cacophony of color nearby. This is a space for outdoor dining, sunbathing, reading, or just lounging. The fast-growing privet hedge can be clipped and trimmed to achieve a wall-like effect that would afford even more privacy.

The back garden provides yet another layer of screening while offering space to grow unusual trees and shrubs. All of the mixed

Plants for a Naturalistic Garden

WOODY PLANTS

Ag: *Acer griseum*

Am: Dutchman's pipe (*Aristolochia macrophylla*)

Bd: Butterfly bush (*Buddleia davidii* 'Dartmoor')

Ca: *Clethra alnifolia* 'Hummingbird'

CaE: Redtwig dogwood (*Cornus alba* 'Elegantissima')

Cd: Beautyberry (*Callicarpa dichotoma*)

Cj: Katsura tree (*Cercidiphyllum japonicum*)

Cl: Yellowwood (*Cladrastis lutea*)

Co: False cypress (*Chamaecyparis obtusa* 'Fastigiata')

Cm: *Clematis maximowicziana*

CmG: Cornelian cherry (*Cornus mas* 'Golden Glory')

Cp: Sweet fern (*Comptonia peregrina*)

CsS: Red osier dogwood (*Cornus sericea* 'Silver and Gold')

Cv: *Clematis viticella* 'Etoile Violette'

Dc: *Daphne caucasica*

FW: *Forsythia* 'Winterthur'

Ha: *Hydrangea anomola* var. *petiolaris*

HqS: *Hydrangea quercifolia* 'Snow Queen'

HyG: *Hydrangea paniculata* 'Grandiflora'

Ic: Japanese holly (*Ilex crenata* 'Sky Pencil')

LG: Woodbine (*Lonicera periclymenum* 'Graham Thomas')

Lo: California privet (*Ligustrum ovalifolium*)

RP: *Rhododendron* 'PJM'

Sj: Japanese skimmia (*Skimmia japonica*)

SrS: European red elder (*Sambucus racemosa* 'Sutherland Gold')

St: Thunberg spirea (*Spiraea thunbergii*)

ToP: Oriental arborvitae (*Thuja orientalis* 'Pyramidalis')

ToS: Arborvitae (*Thuja occidentalis* 'Smaragd')

VdE: *Viburnum dilatatum* 'Erie'

HERBACEOUS PLANTS

Gl: *Gaura lindheimeri* 'Siskiyou Pink'

Gm: *Geranium macrorrhizum* 'Ingwersen's Variety'

HP: *Hosta* 'Patriot'

HpG: *Hosta plantaginea* var. *grandiflora*

HS: *Hosta* 'Sum and Substance'

Ky: *Kalimeris yomena* 'Variegata'

KL: Red-hot poker (*Kniphofia* 'Little Maid')

Pa: Fountain grass (*Pennisetum alopecuroides* 'Hameln')

Ps: *Patrinia scabiosifolia*

PvC: Switch grass (*Panicum virgatum* 'Cloud Nine')

Ss: *Sedum spectabile*

Vb: *Verbena bonariensis*

shrub borders have perennials incorporated into them to extend the flowering season and to create dynamic and ever-changing floral tapestries.

The cost of the stone terrace would be approximately $10,000, the pergola $5,000, the pea gravel $400, the containers $600, the garden furniture $2,500, the soil preparation $3,000, and the plants $3,500. Being hands-on gardeners, the clients choose to do their own planting.

Since most of the shrubs are fast-growing, the clients could purchase smaller plants and use the money saved to buy larger, more mature examples of the slow-growing specimen trees in the planting plan. These showy woody plants will serve as important visual anchors and are integral to the design.

Two avid gardeners will be able to maintain this garden themselves. The plants chosen for the design are easy to grow and don't require anything special in terms of maintenance or care. Once the garden is planted, the only part that will require intensive work is the privet hedge, which will need to be sheared several times over the course of the growing season. Mulch would be used on all borders. This garden should knit together to create a satisfactory whole when the trees and shrubs mature three to five years after planting. After 10 years, when the mature garden provides even greater privacy, I would suggest removing the privet hedge. With minimal maintenance a goal as our clients age, this area could then be converted to lawn.

SCOTT LANKFORD
Water Gardens Are a Focal Point in this Formal Garden

I designed this garden to extend my clients' usable living space and to create a place for them to indulge their developing fascination with water plants. I also wanted the garden to echo some of the formal elements of their home's architecture. The backyard is divided into three spaces linked by a gently curved stone pathway. To keep the design from being too formal, I used mossy stone to give the water garden and its surroundings a more naturalistic look.

I linked the formal style of the house directly to the garden by adding a trellis, a hedge-enclosed herb garden, a patio for entertaining, and more formal plantings, including a pairing of false cypress.

Directly off the patio lie two ponds, which can be seen from inside the house. Here, the path leads between the ponds and over a small bridge, which spans a dry streambed. To construct the ponds, I chose a more durable hard-shell system, as opposed to a flexible liner. I'll cover the pond's unsightly edge with a coping of cobblestones laid right around the lip.

The most formal plantings are adjacent to the structures. Farther away from the built elements, the plants become progressively wilder in form.

Beyond the bridge, the path threads a small area of trees and shrubs, then passes under a trellis before ending at a formal grid of timber-edged raised beds that serves as a showcase for the clients' perennial collection. The beds are laid out for ease of maintenance, with plenty of pathway for maneuvering wheelbarrows and such. The height of the beds means that the clients won't have to kneel down so far to tend their plantings, and it also brings a strong sense of form and structure to the garden when the beds are bare in winter.

To add privacy and enclosure, I used a mixture of lath screens, fencing, and trellises. Using a variety of materials makes the yard seem larger. To subtly separate the ponds from the raised beds in the back, I used large screening plantings of smoke bush and Portuguese laurel. The other plantings in this area are layered to hide

the bottoms of the plants just behind them. The tiered effect makes it seems as if the planting bed is much deeper than it really is.

Adding vertical elements was crucial to the success of the pond area, and the upright foliage provided by irises and ornamental grasses prevents the backyard from seeming far too flat.

To bring a bright, "cottagey" feel to the garden, I included floriferous shrubs such as the doublefile viburnum and hydrangea and colorful perennials like bee balm, astilbe, cardinal flower, daylilies, and lavenders. The borders are edged with coral bells, sweet woodruff, and Japanese holly. To me, an important element of a garden is fragrance, which I tried to introduce with the Japanese snowbell, lavender, cardinal flower, fothergilla, and pieris.

I envision building this garden in stages. First will be grading the site and excavating soil for the ponds. Then the hardscape and structures—raised beds, trellises, the shed, paths, drainage, and irrigation—can be installed. Most of this phase is too difficult for homeowners, so hiring a crew will be a necessity. But there are plenty of able, handy clients skilled

enough to lay the paver patio and stone walks and to do the necessary carpentry. Obviously, that would mean significant savings.

Assuming the hardscape and ponds are built by professionals, constructing the patio and pergola will cost $4,000 to $4,800. The fencing and trellis work at the edge of the property should cost about $1,600. The two ponds could be built, lined, and coped with stones for about $6,000; the bridge will add another $800. The stone walkways, built of concrete cast in place, will cost $1,200. In the far back part of the yard, building the tool shed and raised beds should run about $3,000—more if the shed is to be beyond a basic storage area.

To save money, I've planned for the clients to do the soil preparation, plant buying, and planting. They can expect to spend about $3,000 to finish the garden.

I planned for the garden to fill in within three years and be knit tightly together in five. It should last, without major modifications, for about 25 years.

Though the clients are avid gardeners, their time constraints made low maintenance a crucial element for this garden. The plants selected were chosen for their suitability to the existing conditions and for their ability to create a harmonious community. Ongoing maintenance will simply be a matter of deadheading flowers, occasional watering, minor pruning and putting down a layer of mulch each fall. The pond should require minimal maintenance, as the hard-shell types don't need attention and plants can be grown in submerged containers. I did not design it to be a fish pond; having koi would add a lot of work and in my experience, the fish really tend to chew up pond plants. The installation of an automatic irrigation system with pond fillers to top off the water gardens would help further reduce maintenance. That would add another $3,500 to the overall cost.

"To bring a bright, 'cottagey' feel to the garden, I included floriferous shrubs."—Scott Lankford

Plants for a Formal Garden

1 Japanese snowbell (*Styrax japonicum*)
2 Sourwood (*Oxydendrum arboreum*)
3 Doublefile viburnum (*Viburnum plicatum* f. *tomentosum*)
4 *Hydrangea macrophylla* 'Nikko Blue'
5 'Olympic Fire' mountain laurel (*Kalmia latifolia* 'Olympic Fire')
6 'Mountain Flame' Japanese pieris (*Pieris japonica* 'Mountain Flame')
7 Box blueberry (*Vaccinium ovatum*)
8 Portugal laurel (*Prunus lusitanica*)
9 Sweet woodruff (*Galium odoratum*)
10 'Bluecrop' highbush blueberry (*Vaccinium corymbosum* 'Bluecrop')
11 Sweet box (*Sarcococca ruscifolia*)
12 *Rhododendron* 'Taurus'
13 *Miscanthus sinensis* 'Gracillimus'
14 'Royal Purple' smoke tree (*Cotinus coggygria* 'Royal Purple')
15 'Blue Mist' dwarf fothergilla (*Fothergilla gardenii* 'Blue Mist')
16 *Viburnum davidii*
17 'Munstead' lavender (*Lavandula angustifolia* 'Munstead')
18 'Cambridge Scarlet' bee balm (*Monarda didyma* 'Cambridge Scarlet')
19 'Green Island' Japanese holly (*Ilex crenata* 'Green Island')
20 Astilbe 'Purplelanze'
21 Japanese iris (*Iris ensata*)
22 Stella D'Oro daylily (*Hemerocallis* 'Stella D'Oro')
23 Coral bells (*Heuchera sanguinea*)
24 'Nana Gracilus' false cypress (*Chamaecypris obtusa* 'Nana Gracilus')
25 'Compliment Scarlet' cardinal flower (*Lobelia cardinalis* 'Compliment Scarlet')
26 Beach strawberry (*Fragaria chiloensis*)
27 Water iris (*Iris pseudacorus*)
28 Skunk cabbage (*Lysichiton americanus*)
29 'Mr. Lincoln' hybrid tea rose (*Rosa* 'Mr. Lincoln')
30 'Hidcote' lavender (*Lavandula angustifolia* 'Hidcote')

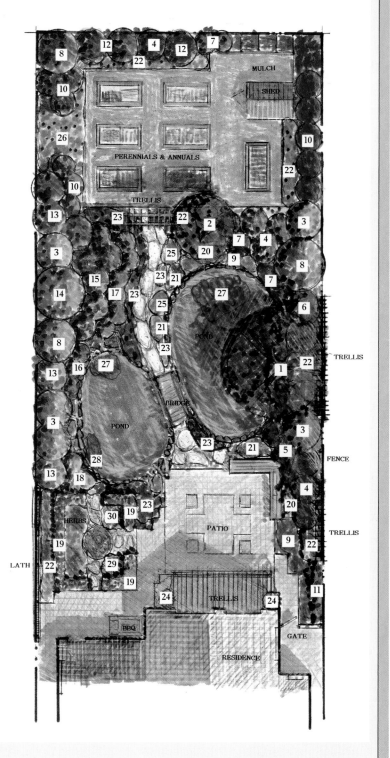

KEVIN J. DOYLE

is a garden designer and lecturer in Dover, Massachusetts. His garden, Cairn Croft, has been featured on The Garden Conservancy Tour and *The Victory Garden.*

Pathways...
Invitations to
Explore

Pathways provide access to the garden. This mahogany footbridge spans a pond, leading from a cultivated hillside garden to a natural woodland trail.

I ALWAYS ENJOY WATCHING first-time visitors to my garden when they reach the cobbled path that disappears into the pond. They just stand there, peering into the water. Intrigued, they want to know where the path leads. Since the level of my pond fluctuates throughout the year, I built a path to the bottom. This way, no matter how low the water level drops, the path will always lead to the water's edge.

Pathways have become the threads that weave together the diverse topography of my garden, giving access to many areas that would otherwise be difficult to reach. A drumlin, my property rises as an elongate hill from the surrounding valley, with the house sitting peacefully at the top. From this high point, the land descends dramatically in every direction over rocky outcroppings. At the bottom rests a pond and stream with broad, boggy shoulders. And beyond the wetlands lies a mixed New England woodland.

A cobbled path disappears mysteriously into the pond, giving access to the water's edge even as the water level drops throughout the year.

It is a delightful place to garden, but without pathways, it might easily resemble an obstacle course.

Pathways also link my garden visually. I am, at heart, a plant collector, so these paths tie together the eclectic collection of flowering trees, conifers, shrubs, grasses, bulbs, and herbaceous plants that I've assembled through the years.

THINK OF YOUR DRIVEWAY AS A PATH

I live along a country road, which thoughtfully winds its way through a stand of mature hardwoods, around large stone outcroppings, and beyond a small pond. Unlike newer roads—which are often created through a process of blasting, filling, and leveling—this path-of-old makes its way through the natural terrain as best it can. I took my first lesson from this old road as I designed my initial path, the driveway. After being greeted by two cairns that flank the entrance, visitors wind their way up the hillside and through the trees, carefully skirting several boulders. Cairns are conical heaps of stone used as landmarks on mountain trails. Here, these piles of indigenous rock serve as beacons, inviting guests to my home and garden, which I call Cairn Croft.

The drive is laid in crushed gravel, 12 in. deep for a solid base, and is topped with a 2-in. dressing of buff-colored pea stone. A brick edge holds the stone in place and provides contrast in texture and color. Either under foot or under tire, the pleasant crunch of gravel announces the arrival of visitors to my home.

THE SIZE OF A PATH HINTS AT ITS IMPORTANCE

Near the house, a parking area doubles as a forecourt. Plants casually spill out of the surrounding gardens, greeting guests as they arrive. Here, visitors have a choice among two paths. Odd as it may sound, the smaller, less formal path winds its way to the front door, while the dominant, more explicit path leads straight to the garden. The reason is simple: More people visit my garden than my home, and my garden is the grander of the two.

The path to my front door is simple, but enticing. After three tries at creating a typical suburban lawn, I turned my efforts to designing an enhanced forest floor to better blend with my home's natural surroundings. A narrow path, it is laid with indigenous stepping-stones set on an 8-in. bed of gravel. The stones are tucked into place with topsoil and mulch. Heavily planted to mimic a pathway through a lush woodland, it passes a cozy resting place where a small pool of water and a pair of old, iron garden seats suggest a pause.

The more formal path leads to the garden. Because I wanted to draw attention to this entrance, it is 5 ft. wide and flanked by two granite piers. The grade changes, so steps were added. Borrowing from the front walkway theme, three large, indigenous, flat stepping-stones were set in place, with cobblestones filling in and squaring off the space. This pleasant juxtaposition of natural and man-made give the area a crafted character.

LET PLANTS SPILL INTO GARDEN PATHS

Beyond the entry, the main garden path proceeds in brown pea stone about 2 in. deep, laid on a bed of compressed stone dust. For walkways, I have found the stone dust easier to work with than crushed gravel. It can be maneuvered by wheelbarrow and compacts nicely with water, forming a sturdy base. The pea stone is bordered by rounded stones of about softball size that hold the smaller bits of stone in place and lend a rustic appearance to the trail.

Along the way, I encourage a few plants to creep from the borders into the path in a deliberate but natural way. Here, I have also planted spring-flowering bulbs and all manner of small plants that thrive on quick drainage and in dry conditions. *Sedum, Sempervivum, Thymus, Allium,* and *Arenaria* species dot the edges of the path—sometimes singly, but more often in small groups. Self-sowing species, such as *Lychnis* and *Alchemilla,* also sneak into the gravel. To keep these creepers under con-trol and maintain a passable walk, judicious weeding is done early in the season.

Where the grade steepens, I have built steps with short risers and deep treads to keep the transitions gentle. Most of my steps are 3 or 4 ft. wide to allow for comfortable passage. The risers are made of large, rounded boulders with flat tops that I collected during daily forays into the country. I am always on the lookout for stones, for I have discovered that it is essential to have extra stone on hand before starting any new project. This permits a good selection throughout the construction process. It's also wise to have a little patience, for fitting irregularly shaped stones together is akin to assembling a puzzle.

TRAVERSE A STEEP HILLSIDE

Along the path to the rear of the property, the grade is much steeper. I was confronted with two challenges in negotiating the slope that runs to the pond. The first was to provide a comfortable walk from top to bottom. The second was to afford access to as much of the

An intimate path leads visitors to the house through a heavily planted area designed to blend into the natural surroundings.

garden as possible. The solution was a path that traversed the slope like a hiking trail, making the descent ever so gentle and bringing the viewer across the garden. Near the end of this crisscrossing path, where the slope drops dramatically, a few steps improve access.

At this point, a sloping lawn flows from the backyard like a green river headed for the pond below. This grassy river acts as a path of its own, deliberately guiding visitors to the junction of the path and stairs. Here, an old porch baluster stands as a trail marker. Beyond the steps, the path twists quickly out of sight as it approaches the pond crossing.

EXPLORE THE WETLANDS AND WOODLANDS ON NATURAL PATHS

The bridge over the pond was inspired by a pair of existing stone peninsulas that had provided passage for nearly a century. A couple of old logs joined the peninsulas, creating a footbridge. A lovely composition, I took guidance

Paths whose final destination is hidden create a sense of mystery.

Containers can be placed along a path for added interest.

Meandering paths, as compared to straight paths, create a more naturalistic setting.

Selected plants are encouraged to creep into paths in a deliberate but natural way.

The edges of this path are softened and hidden by plants.

from the union of stone and wood, enhancing it for safety and comfort. After stabilizing the piers with additional rock, I built a simple mahogany bridge over the channel. For me, this crossing serves as a reminder that it is the journey, and not the destination, that should be savored.

Upstream, a couple of cedar logs and old, rough hewn planks straddle a narrow spot for crossing. Because the ground is soft and boggy, a series of irregularly placed stepping-stones lead garden visitors safely from the footbridge to solid ground.

Across the pond, the tenor of the garden changes. Contrasting with the highly cultivated, colorful, and stone-clad hillside, a simple path of mulch and wood chips invites you to walk quietly through the forest. For the most part, I've left the woods to the hands of Mother Nature. A stroll through these woodlands is soothing and peaceful.

There are two paths on this side of the pond. A short path circles the pond intimately, offering brief glimpses of the house, garden, and aviary. The longer path winds its way over a knoll and outcropping, toward the perimeter of the property, and then back again to the stream crossing. Bells of various sizes and tones hang in the trees along this path. Visitors strike them while wandering through the forest, alerting me to their whereabouts. I have always thought the garden was at its best with people in it. When I hear the soft, deep resonance of the bells, I know the garden is engaged, even though I can't see anyone.

Much of this forest pathway is little more than woodland duff; most of the plantings are natural. Yet, by placing occasional artifacts and statuary fragments in unexpected locations, I've created an element of intrigue for the observant passerby. In fact, for some visitors, it almost becomes a treasure hunt.

Enjoy a quiet walk in the woods along this lightly mulched path. Forest garden design has been left in the hands of Mother Nature.

A wooden footbridge and stepping-stones provide safe passage over the stream and through the swamp.

Paths are practical matters, helping you get from place to place. But what I enjoy most about creating a path is staging the scenery along the way. You see, the garden is like my own little amphitheater. I come to life and perform here, and my paths guide you through the yarn I am spinning.

"What I enjoy most about creating a path is staging the scenery along the way."

LINDA GOLYMBIESKI

is co-owner of Apia Garden Restoration, a landscape design firm. Many of the firm's designs have been featured on garden tours that raise funds to preserve open space in Connecticut.

Planting *a* Playground

(LEFT) Jessica and Tara never tire of watching each other draw.

(INSET) Pieces of bluestone serve as chalkboards.

AS KIDS, my business partner, Claudia D'Occhio, and I spent our days climbing trees, hunting for fossils, and feasting on berries we found growing wild in the woods. Imagining life as an adult was just another game to play. Now that we're grown, we still cherish our childlike sense of play and wonder. So, we were delighted when some of our clients, who, like us, had not lost their sense of childhood adventure, came up with a unique project. They wanted us to create a place their two young daughters could call their own—a garden and play space whimsical and interactive enough for the children to like, but sophisticated enough to look appealing from the house and the street.

It wasn't exactly child's play, but we developed a design featuring a semicircular berm, kidproof perennials, Dr. Seusslike oddball plants, berries for snacking, playful paths, and all kinds of fun things. From the house it would look like an attractive planting. From the road, it would look like a perennial garden. And from the inside, it looks like, well, a playground.

MAKE THE MOST OF THE EXISTING SITE

The site we selected for the new garden was already landscaped. It had an oval bed with a beautiful, 10-ft. blue spruce, a dozen sun-baked mountain laurels, two immovable rock formations, and a thick layer of pine mulch. It also had a full sun exposure, perfect for flowering perennials and children at play.

First, we decided what we could keep and what should go. The spruce was too beautiful to move, so we designed around it. The rocks weren't going anywhere, so we decided to incorporate them into the design, too—they were big enough to play on, and we thought the kids might imagine them as a fort, a sailing ship, or the top of Mount Everest. As for the scraggly laurels, we decided to dig them up and transplant them into a more hospitable area.

Because the site was flat, we added interest to it by building a low berm that would also help create a hideaway for the children that could be seen from the house but not from the road. We'd rework the bed into a crescent shape and plant its borders with perennials and a tree for climbing. The interior would be flat and free of plantings so the kids could run and hop and dig. The thought of them hopping through the garden gave us the idea to add a flat field-stone path that would meander through the site. By providing them with a pathway to enter and exit the play area, we hoped to curb their urge to cut through the plantings.

Having been avid tree climbers ourselves, we knew the spruce was too prickly to climb and that the best climbing trees were deciduous, with a low canopy for easy access. We selected a crabapple, *Malus* 'Centurion', whose rose-red spring flowers produce small, glossy, red fruits, providing food for songbirds and winter color. The tree would reach 25 ft. in height and 20 ft. in breadth, with well-spaced branches throughout.

The last element was a fountain, a place where the girls could cool their hands and faces. We searched for something sophisticated enough for adults yet still appealing to chil-

A small berm gives the new bed a sculptural dimension. One of the first steps in the project was creating a long, low mound of earth to help define the garden.

Playgrounds need a tree for climbing. This young crabapple will soon be large enough.

dren and finally found a 2-ft. replica of a grizzly bear standing in a miniature cascade. The bear's black, glassy eyes gave it such a lifelike appearance that we were sure the girls would adopt it as a pet.

CREATE PRIVACY WITH A BERM

Once our clients approved the plans, drawings, and fountain, we set about preparing the site. The bed's original shape was a predictable oval, but we wanted something more dynamic, so we re-edged it to have curving sides and a wider bottom. In the process, we discovered there wasn't an inch of good soil under the heavily mulched bed. Since the soil in this part of Connecticut is a maddening mix of sand, rocks, and more rocks, we ordered plenty of topsoil and compost made especially for perennial garden installations. We had the material dumped in the two berm areas, shoveled and raked it into smooth, mounded hills about 18 in. high, then tamped the soil with our feet. Tamping a new berm before planting is extremely important because air pockets can later cause plantings to heave up and dry out. And since we were putting a climbing tree in the berm, we wanted to be sure that it had a firm bed. After the first tamping, we watered the soil to help it settle more and then tamped it again. By early afternoon we were ready to install the tree and shrubs.

PLANT BERRIES FOR KIDS TO EAT

Recalling the fun we had as kids pretending to forage for food, we decided to incorporate a few edibles into the design. We planted an edging of everbearing strawberries (*Fragaria* spp.) along the outside of the berm, where the fruit would be easy to reach and the plants' runners would be kept in check by the passing lawn mower.

We added blueberry bushes (*Vaccinium* spp.), too. The berries are tasty, and the small,

4- to 5-ft. shrubs have white spring flowers and splendid red fall foliage that makes them a good ornamental choice. We planted them near the spruce, allowing ample room for growth. The 3-ft. plants already had berries on them, which were a welcome treat for the kids that same day.

With the bushes in place near the spruce, the fountain nook was taking shape. Our clients, Jeff and Antonette, had already hired an electrician to install a concealed electrical outlet to provide power for the pump. We wanted to position the fountain in front of the blueberries, and created a foundation for it by slightly excavating the area, tamping the soil, and topping it with a piece of flat bluestone. Then we assembled the fountain, added a pump and water, and plugged it in. A few bits of moss, some sticks, and a few pebbles further enhanced the look of the bubbly cascade. Jessica's and Tara's faces glowed as the miniature waterfall tumbled behind and around the bear's feet and into the tiny, rocky pool below.

Strange-looking plants fascinate children. The spiky, blue balls of rattlesnake master attract lots of attention.

Open space gives kids
room to play.

Low plantings on the
house side allow par-
ents to keep an eye on
the children.

Berms and boulders
add dimension to
the space.

A bear fountain provides the sound of trickling water.

Deep plantings buffer the garden from the road.

Flowers make the playspace a cheerful setting and attract butterflies.

> *"To add whimsy to the design, we included a few of our favorite 'weirdo' plants."*

Kids love butterflies, so be sure to include plants that will attract the fluttering insects. This coneflower captured the attention of a silver-spotted skipper.

Each day brings new surprises for children exploring the garden. Jessica surveys the garden almost every day to see what new flowers are in bloom.

They promptly christened her Sunshine and tried to feed her a blueberry!

We placed two large, rectangular, bluestone pieces on the inside slope of the berm to serve as drawing boards for the children. Next, we laid out the irregular stone "hopping path." The stones were closely laid to accommodate a child's stride and surrounded by mulch. The path was then tamped down during a hopping contest between Claudia and me, with Jessica not far behind.

USE CURIOSITIES AS ACCENTS

The following day we planted perennials and ornamental grasses. We chose tough plants that would stand up to children, but they also had to be long-flowering and relatively maintenance-free. Switch grasses—*Panicum virgatum* 'Heavy Metal', an upright, metallic-blue grass that grows 3 to 4 ft., and *P. virgatum* 'Haense Herms', a taller, less rigid variety, topping 5 ft., with a remarkable red color in fall—were planted on the side of the garden that faced the road, creating a hidden world for the girls but one that gave their parents a clear view of them from the house.

We tried to select perennials that would interest any child. For early spring color, we installed *Geranium maculatum* 'Spessart', a standout with apple-scented leaves in compact mounds and tiny, light pink flower clusters that last for months. We also added 'Moonbeam' coreopsis (*Coreopsis verticillata* 'Moonbeam'), an airy herbaceous mound virtually covered in child-size stars of lemon-yellow from June through frost.

Since Jessica has a passion for butterflies, adding perennials that would attract them was a must. We used 'Bright Star' coneflowers (*Echinacea purpurea* 'Bright Star') for its pink beacons, long-flowering *Salvia* × *superba* 'Blue Queen', and *Liatris scariosa* 'September Glory', whose 3-ft., red-violet spikes are an especially welcome sight in late August.

To add whimsy to the design, we included a few of our favorite "weirdo" plants. Rattlesnake master (*Eryngium yuccifolium*) is a striking plant that bears fragrant 1½-in., golf ball–like flower heads on 3-ft. stalks. We also added giant alliums (*Allium giganteum*), with their softball-sized heads, and redhot pokers (*Kniphofia* 'Alcazar'), bearing sturdy 40-in. stalks tipped with red, flame-shaped heads that attract the attention of both children and hummingbirds.

At the base of the fountain, we worked in the sun-loving *Hosta* 'Sum and Substance'—its giant chartreuse leaves can reach to 3 ft. across—which we hoped would help to create a fairy-tale setting. Along the hopping path and framing the bluestone drawing boards, we added a host of hens-and-chicks (*Sempervivum* spp.). Their tough little rosettes are as child-proof as a prescription bottle.

THE GARDEN MATURES ALONG WITH THE CHILDREN

Part of the beauty of our design is in its ever-changing nature. Over time, some elements can be altered to suit the clients' evolving taste without compromising the entire scheme.

Anticipating the garden's growth with good soil preparation and proper spacing of plants ensures the success of the design as well. As it matures, plants can be divided and shared, seeds can be given away, berries can be preserved, furnishings can be added or removed. In time, this garden may seem smaller than Jessica and Tara once believed it to be, but we hope that in their memories it will remain forever boundless.

A peaceful perch for reading or playing, this rustic-looking bench is within earshot of the gentle sound of the bear fountain and not too far from a blueberry bush.

Credits

PHOTOS

Front matter
Lee Anne White, © The Taunton Press, Inc.—p. ii
© J. Paul Moore—p. iii
© Ken Druse; © Charles Mann; © Ken Druse; Lee Anne White, © The Taunton Press, Inc. (top); Steve Silk, © The Taunton Press, Inc. (bottom)—Contents (from left)
© John Glover—p. 2

Part I: Getting Started
Lee Anne White, © The Taunton Press, Inc.—pp. 4–6, 8, 10–11, 14–17, 22–24 (#s 1–10, 12–19), 25–28, 38–40, 42, 43
Steve Silk, © The Taunton Press, Inc.—pp. 22 (#11), 24 (#20)
Scott Phillips, © The Taunton Press, Inc.—pp. 30, 36
© Ken Druse—pp. 44, 46, 47, 49, 50
Virginia Small, © The Taunton Press, Inc.—p. 45 (author)

Part II: Creative Approaches
© J. Paul Moore—pp. 53, 54, 67–72, 74 (right), 76
© John Glover—pp. 52, 56–58, 61
© Roger Foley—p. 59 (top)
© Paddy Wales—pp. 59 (bottom), 83 (top)
Lee Anne White, © The Taunton Press, Inc.—pp. 62 (garden of Ryan Gainey, Decatur, Ga.), 64 (garden of Kim Hawks, Chapel Hill, N.C.), 65 (garden of Susanne and Roger Schlaifer, Atlanta, Ga.), 66 (garden of Jim Stobbs, Canton, Ga.), 92, 94, 95, 97–99
© Sharon Densmore—p. 74 (top left and top bottom)
© Darrel G. Morrison—p. 78
© Susan Roth—pp. 80 (left), 82 (left)
© David McDonald—pp. 80 (right), 81 (top), 82 (right), 83 (bottom)
© Charles Mann—p. 81 (bottom)
Delilah Smittle, © The Taunton Press, Inc.—pp. 84, 86, 88, 89, 91
© Rick Darke—pp. 100, 102, 103, 105, 106 (top)
Virginia Small, © The Taunton Press, Inc.—p. 106 (bottom)

Part III: Front Yard Ideas
© Allan Mandell—pp. 108, 126, 129, 130
Susan Kahn, © The Taunton Press, Inc.—pp. 109, 131, 132
Delilah Smittle, © The Taunton Press, Inc.—pp. 136, 138, 140, 141
Steve Silk, © The Taunton Press, Inc.—pp. 142, 144, 145 (top), 146, 147
© Bert Klassen—p. 145 (inset)

Part IV: Gallery of Ideas
© Allan Mandell—pp. 148, 150, 153, 154
Lee Anne White, © The Taunton Press, Inc.—pp. 149, 155–159, 160 (top), 170, 172–175
© Laura Lenox—p. 160 (bottom right)
Steve Silk, © The Taunton Press, Inc.—pp. 160 (bottom left), 176–183

ILLUSTRATIONS
Jeni Webber—pp. 12, 17, 18, 20, 21, 162, 163
Jodie Delohery—pp. 26, 27, 29
C. Colston Burrell—pp. 32–34
Mahan Rykiel Associates, Inc.—p. 41
Melanie Magee—pp. 46–47
Vince Babak—pp. 56, 86, 87, 96, 165
Courtesy *The Architecture of Country Houses*—p. 59
Peter Eckert—pp. 60, 61
Michelle Burchard—pp. 70–71, 73
Gwendolyn Babbitt—pp. 110, 112, 114–116
Gary Williamson—pp. 118, 120–122, 124, 133
Marc Vassallo—p. 151
Gary Keim—p. 166
Scott Lankford—pp. 168, 169